Retailing Smarts

providing personalized customer service

CRISP
PUBLICATIONS

Retailing Smarts

Providing Personalized Customer Service

Credits:

Senior Editor:	Debbie Woodbury
Design and Layout:	Brandi Sladek
Production Manager:	Judy Petry
Cartoonist:	James McFarlane
Advisor:	Margery Steinberg, Ph.D.

Based on materials by Robert Taggart, Ph.D., Remediation & Training Institute
Editorial services provided by Watershed Books

Copyright ©1999 by Crisp Publications, Inc.
Printed in the United States of America by Bawden Printing Company
Crisp Publications internet address: www.crisp-pub.com

98 99 00 01   10 9 8 7 6 5 4 3 2 1

Library of Congress Catalog Card Number 98-074370
ISBN 1-56052-518-5
Crisp editors, based on material by Robert Taggart
Providing Personalized Customer Service

This book is printed
on recycled
paper with
soy ink

PRINTED WITH
SOY INK

A Word from the National Retail Federation

The National Retail Federation is pleased to present the *Retailing Smarts* series. These books represent a whole new approach to developing training and educational materials based on national skill standards. Topics and information covered in these books reflect what retail employers across the country agree is needed to succeed and grow in a retail career.

We are proud of helping the retail industry pioneer the development of skill standards and raise expectations for a committed and competitive workforce. The *Retailing Smarts* series sets a new standard for industry-driven education and training that leads to productive and measurable results.

We encourage you to use this series and to let us know how these books are helpful to you, as a large or small company, or as an individual student or worker. With your feedback, the National Retail Federation can continue to create and improve the educational and training products that our industry needs to advance.

Tracy Mullin

Tracy Mullin
President
National Retail Federation

A Word from the National Retail Institute

The National Retail Institute, the non-profit research and education foundation of the National Retail Federation, is committed to creating the next generation of retail workers with competitive skills and career options.

The *Retailing Smarts* series will help retail workers develop the skills they need to perform well on the job and to take advantage of the range of options retailing can provide. We believe this series will help promote the image and opportunities — and recognize the professionalism and talents of those who make retailing a career.

W.R. Howell
Chairman Emeritus, J.C. Penney Company
Chairman, National Retail Institute

Remediation & Training Institute

Providing Personalized Customer Service is based on materials developed by Robert Taggart, Ph.D., President of the Remediation & Training Institute. The nonprofit institute, based in Alexandria, Virginia, develops educational and training courseware, tools, and model programs and conducts basic research and program evaluations.

Dr. Taggart developed the nationally-recognized Comprehensive Competencies Program, a public-use system for delivering individualized self-paced, competency-based instruction covering K-12 academics and all functional skills.

From the Carter administration to the present, Dr. Taggart has served as an advocate for disadvantaged and minority groups, particularly youth, in shaping policy and educational initiatives. He is a prolific researcher and author, as well as an innovative social program developer.

Contents

Introduction

Part 1: Get To Know Your Customer

Part 2: Meet Your Customers' Needs

Part 3: Build a Continuing Relationship

Contents (cont.)

introduction

The Retailing Smarts Series

Welcome to *Retailing Smarts*, a collection of learning materials developed specifically for the retail sales associate by Crisp Publications and the National Retail Federation (NRF), the world's largest retail association. The *Retailing Smarts* series is designed to provide training for the national retail skill standards, which were developed under the leadership of the NRF. Thanks to a collaboration of representatives from all types and sizes of retailers, the concepts, examples and skill practice activities in the *Retailing Smarts* series are applicable across the retail industry.

Retailing Smarts provides a fun and easy way to learn and practice retailing skills in a self-study format. The materials can also be adapted by educators and training professionals for use in the classroom or corporate training programs.

Providing Personalized Customer Service is one of the six major NRF skill standard categories, as listed below.

- ☑ Providing Personalized Customer Service
- ❑ Selling and Promoting Products
- ❑ Monitoring Inventory
- ❑ Maintaining the Store
- ❑ Protecting Company Assets
- ❑ Working as a Team

A Roadmap to Success: Retail Skill Standards

What trainers need to teach, what workers need to learn, what employers can expect.

What are skill standards?

Skill standards provide workers with a clear definition of what they need to know and do to be successful on the job. The retail skill standards describe the tasks involved for sales associates in the retail profession. They also describe how professional sales associates should behave in carrying out those tasks. This means workers now have a roadmap for understanding what is expected of them, how their performance is being measured, and what they need to learn to become proficient at their jobs.

Skill standards also provide a basis for selecting and training a skilled workforce. Employers use these standards to evaluate a candidate's level of experience and accomplishment in the skills that apply to their business. Employers and educators use skill standards to train people in a specific industry. This education may begin in a classroom setting, either prior to employment (as in high school, trade schools, or college) or in classes conducted by employers for workers they have already hired. Training in skill standards can also be accomplished by individuals who are willing to study on their own, using resources like this book.

Whether in a classroom or through self-study, learning about retail skill standards is only the beginning of the journey. Along the way, experiences with customers and co-workers will increase the understanding and mastery of these skills. Since each day brings new experiences, what began as training becomes lifelong learning. And when a person continues to learn, there is no limit to the successes he or she can achieve.

A Roadmap to Success: Retail Skill Standards (cont.)

How were the retail skill standards developed?

Since 1992, hundreds of retailers, educators, and government representatives have participated in the development of skill standards for the retail industry, led by the National Retail Federation. This is part of a larger effort to define skill standards for all industry segments in conjunction with the National Skills Standards Board.

The initial retail skill standards have been developed for the professional sales associate for several reasons:

- The majority of North American workers enters the workforce through a job in the retail industry.

- The skills required for success in these entry-level positions are the same skills that will help workers succeed throughout their lives, both personally and professionally, whether in the retail industry or some other field of work or profession.

- In our current service-oriented and global economy, retailers need to attract and retain a dedicated, competitive retail workforce.

Which skill standards are addressed in this series?

The following retail skill sub-categories are addressed in *Providing Personalized Customer Service:*

- Initiate Customer Contact

- Build Customer Relations

A detailed list of the key tasks associated with these skills is provided on the next page.

Skill Standards for Providing Personalized Customer Service

Skill Set: Initiate Customer Contact

In this book you will learn how to apply the following skill standards:

✔ Determine customer's needs by listening and asking questions: Part 1

✔ Make shopping experience enjoyable for customers: Part 2

✔ Give customer an appropriate greeting: Part 1

✔ Inform customer of additional services: Part 2

✔ Refer customer to another department or store: Part 1

Skill Set: Build Customer Relations

✔ Follow through on commitments made to customers: Part 2

✔ Respond to personal needs of shoppers: Part 2

✔ Honor manufacturers' warranties: Part 3

✔ Adhere to company's return policy: Part 3

✔ Handle customer complaints: Part 3

✔ Balance responsive phone service with in-store service: Part 2

✔ Maintain key information on customers: Part 4

✔ Conduct customer follow-up: Part 4

✔ Provide customer with personalized business card: Part 4

✔ Complete special orders: Part 2

✔ Schedule personal appointment with shopper; select merchandise in advance: Part 4

How to Use this Book

Each section of *Providing Customer Service* is divided into several lessons. You may choose to complete only those that directly apply to your retail situation or you may complete all of the lessons to ensure a well-rounded education in the national retail skill standards. The lessons are designed to take less than 30 minutes each to complete. A skill practice is included in most lessons.

Studies show that adults retain new skills more effectively if they apply them immediately to their own experiences. After you have completed the reading and any applicable skill practices for each lesson, put the materials aside and consider how you will apply this information to your work as a professional retail sales associate. If possible, practice this skill on the job before you start another lesson.

If you are using these materials...

On your own:

Find a mentor—an experienced retail sales associate—who will serve as your guide or counselor. After you complete a lesson, review your skill practice responses with this mentor to get additional advice and discuss any questions you may have. A mentor can help you find success in a new career.

Use the Learning Checklists in each section to record your progress. You may even want to have your mentor initial the dates that you complete the skill practices. This completed checklist can provide strong evidence of your commitment to learning when you apply for that first retail position. Potential employers will appreciate your dedication to self-improvement!

As part of a class:

The Learning Checklists can be used by you and your instructor to monitor your progress as you work through the lessons. The instructor may want to review your responses to the skill practices and initial that you have successfully completed each lesson.

How to Use this Book (cont.)

If you are using these materials...
(cont.)

On the job:

The Learning Checklists can be used in two ways if you are using these materials as on-the-job training.

First, your supervisor or a co-worker can observe your actions and initial the date on which you successfully demonstrated specific skills or behaviors. Including a brief description of how you demonstrated the skill will provide a basis for performance evaluation discussions.

Second, the completed checklist and notes about demonstrated skills can provide evidence that you are experienced in the national retail skill standards, reinforcing your credentials as a professional sales associate.

Life-Long Benefits of a Career in Retail

Providing personalized customer service is job number one for sales associates. This is true whether you work in a large department store, a Mom and Pop grocery store, a trendy boutique or the local discount store. Customer service is what makes the difference in whether customers buy tires from you or your competitor, eat at your restaurant or the one across the street, see you for home improvement needs or order from a catalog. Therefore, the position of sales associate is much more than a "cashier" or a "clerk."

The retail sales associate is a professional—a person with specialized knowledge, expertise, and "people skills." The professional sales associate is an expert in customer relations. These experts are in big demand by retailers and through use of their expertise, can turn even an entry-level, routine job into an exciting and rewarding career. And being an expert at customer relations can bring you many other rewards. On the facing page check those which are important to you.

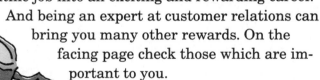

A career in retail has many potential benefits. Check (✓) all of the following that are important to you.

- ❑ Opportunity to help people
- ❑ Flexible working hours
- ❑ Opportunity for promotion
- ❑ Employee discounts on purchases
- ❑ Ability to relocate and still stay in your profession
- ❑ Status as an expert on products and services
- ❑ Personal benefits such as health insurance
- ❑ On-the-job training that is transferable to other fields
- ❑ Ability to choose your work environment
- ❑ Paid vacation
- ❑ Selling products related to personal interests or hobbies
- ❑ Being first to know about new trends and products
- ❑ Meeting new people
- ❑ Learning about other retail functions such as purchasing, display, and store operations
- ❑ On-the-job preparation for starting your own business

You have the potential for all of these benefits and more by becoming an expert in customer relations—and it isn't hard to do! In fact, you are already on your way because you can use your experience as a shopper to develop your skills at helping other customers. However, knowing what satisfies you as a customer is only the beginning of understanding the individual needs and desires of each customer who enters your store. By the time you have read through this book, practiced some of the suggested exercises, and thought about your own experiences, you will be on your way to professional success.

Are you Prepared to Give Quality Service?

Quality customer service means more than following a set of rules. Giving quality service requires developing certain qualities and skills for working with people, gaining their trust, and meeting their needs.

The following exercise will help you learn more about yourself. **It is not a test and you need not share the results with anyone else.** Completing this exercise will help you understand how you currently feel about providing customer service. Answer the questions honestly and the results will help you determine where you need to focus your learning efforts in order to be successful as a sales associate.

skill practice: are you prepared to give quality service?

Directions: circle the number which most closely reflects where you are on the scale for each question. When you're done, add up all the circled numbers and write your score in the space provided below.

No one needs to see your score but you—this exercise is to help you focus your learning efforts and develop the attitude needed to be a successful retail sales associate!

 Feel free to cut this page out of your workbook if you'd like to keep your assessment private.

I control my moods most of the time.	10 9 8 7 6 5 4 3 2 1	I have limited control over my moods.
It is possible for me to be pleasant to people who are in-different to me.	10 9 8 7 6 5 4 3 2 1	I simply can't be pleasant if people are not nice to me.
I like most people and enjoy meeting others.	10 9 8 7 6 5 4 3 2 1	I have difficulties getting along with others.
I enjoy being of service to others.	10 9 8 7 6 5 4 3 2 1	People should help themselves.
I do not mind apologizing for mistakes even if I did not make them.	10 9 8 7 6 5 4 3 2 1	Apologizing for a mistake I didn't make is wrong.
I take pride in my ability to communicate verbally with others.	10 9 8 7 6 5 4 3 2 1	I would rather react with others in writing.
I'm good at remember-ing names and faces, and make efforts to improve this skill when meeting others.	10 9 8 7 6 5 4 3 2 1	Why bother remember-ing a name or face if you will never see that person again?
Smiling comes nat-urally to me.	10 9 8 7 6 5 4 3 2 1	I am more serious by nature.
I like seeing others enjoy themselves.	10 9 8 7 6 5 4 3 2 1	I have no motivation to please others, espe-cially those I don't know.
I keep myself clean and well groomed.	10 9 8 7 6 5 4 3 2 1	Being clean and well groomed is not all that important.

Total score: _____

Understanding Your Self-Assessment

> **"There are a tremendous number of people who work in a retail setting as their first job. The skills they learn on that first job are skills they'll have for the rest of their lives. "**
>
> —Robert B. Reich, former U.S. Secretary of Labor

If you rated yourself 80 or above, you probably are excellent at helping customers. The information in this book will show you how you can refine your skills at meeting customer needs.

If you rated yourself between 30 and 80, you will greatly benefit by using this book to learn more about customer relations.

If you scored under 30, you may want to consider a retail career path that does not involve a lot of customer service. Large retail organizations employ people in functions that keep the company running smoothly, but don't require as much interaction with the general public, such as Distribution or Merchandising.

Even if you should decide at some point that you don't want to work directly with customers on a daily basis, understanding customer service is essential to working well with others. Treating your co-workers like customers will help make you successful in any career you pursue.

part 1

get to know your customer

Be the Store's Frontline Representative

The sales associate is the frontline representative of any retail operation. As such, your first and most important role is to create good relationships with customers. These days, with so many choices of retail stores and products, customers want to come to a store in which salespeople make a special effort to make them feel welcome, respected, and well-served. As one consumer trend expert has written, "Perfect packaging, beautiful product shots, cleverness, style over substance, or hype just don't work anymore."

Sales associates are key . . . This is great news for people who pursue a career in retail sales. It means that stores depend on sales associates, not products or gimmicks, to represent a store's values. And the primary value every good store wants you to communicate is that customers are number one, and that service will be delivered in a personal, one-to-one way. Employers value sales associates who understand and are prepared to give quality customer service.

Learning Checklist for Part 1

As you complete Part 1, *Get to Know Your Customer* record your progress on this checklist. This checklist can also be used as a basis for discussion with your instructor, supervisor, or mentor as you complete the skill practices and/or you demonstrate the specific skills in the workplace.

Lessons completed	Date completed
❑ Lesson 1: Greet Customers in a Winning Way; Create Customer Loyalty	_____
❑ Lesson 2: Build Relationships, One Step at a Time; Be Observant	_____
❑ Lesson 3: Determine a Customer's Needs	_____
❑ Lesson 4: Keep the Lines of Communication Open	_____
❑ Lesson 5: Fit the Products to the Customer	_____
❑ Lesson 6: Offer Alternatives; Know When to Refer a Customer Elsewhere	_____
❑ Roundup	_____

Learning Checklist for Part 1 (cont.)

| Skills Demonstrated in the Workplace | Date Demonstrated |

❏ Give the customer an appropriate greeting _____

Describe the situation and how you demonstrated this skill:

❏ Determine customer's needs by listening _____
and asking questions

Describe the situation and how you demonstrated this skill:

❏ Refer customer to another department _____
or store

Describe the situation and how you demonstrated this skill:

Get to Know Your Customer

Customer service begins the instant someone enters your store. So let's start at the beginning and consider how to greet your customers in a winning way!

LESSON 1

Greet Customers in a Winning Way

> **Most of us form quick first impressions. We often...decide whether we like people, feel good about them, or want to do business with them in those first few seconds of contact.**
>
> —Ron Willingham, author of "Hey, I'm the Customer"

Before you can build a relationship with a customer, you first have to greet the customer in a way that makes her feel welcome and comfortable doing business with you. Some experts say that a sales associate has about ten seconds to notice a customer's arrival and greet her in order to create a good impression. That's not much time, so you need to make every second count.

Your initial greeting should:

1. **Acknowledge the customer's presence**

2. **Project a professional and friendly image**

3. **Create an opening for discussion**

4. **Be reassuring, but not pushy**

5. **Include the entire shopping party**

1. Acknowledge the customer's presence

First of all, don't make a customer wait too long for your attention. Researchers who study customer behavior have learned that if a customer has waited 30 to 40 seconds to be greeted, she is likely to feel she's been waiting three or four minutes. Make eye contact as soon as possible. Even if you are helping another customer, you can excuse yourself briefly and tell the new customer you will be with her in a moment. You can also ask a fellow sales associate to help her. With these thoughtful gestures, you will buy a few more minutes of the customer's patience. Just don't leave her feeling unnoticed. It will make her believe she's going to receive poor service—a first impression that's hard to change.

2. Project a professional and friendly image

Looking professional isn't just about how you dress. It also has to do with acting in an alert and courteous way. Naturally, you need to choose clothing that fits the dress standards of your store—perhaps business wear for a fine apparel store, or casual wear for a hardware store. However, showing the customer you are sincerely interested in serving him is every bit as important in making a positive connection. And a smile is always a direct way to show you're interested and friendly—a smile with both your eyes and your mouth!

Try to greet each new customer in a natural, relaxed way. You might begin by saying something about the rainy weather, for example—"I'll bet you're glad to be in from the weather!" Or you might notice that the customer has a good sense of humor from a funny comment he makes. You can let him know you appreciate what he just said.

Greet Customers in a Winning Way (cont.)

3. Create an opening for discussion

Asking "May I help you?" or "Can I help you find anything?" may set you up for a dead-end response from the customer such as "No, thank you," or "Just looking." Instead, observe the customer to pick up some clues to start a conversation. Establish a common interest between you and the customer. If the customer tries out a product, watch her reaction and make an appropriate comment.

> **Customer:** *"Um, nice lotion."*
>
> **Sales Associate:** *"That's our most popular line; I use the Kiwi version of it myself."*

Or if the customer sits on a mattress to test it and says, "Wow, that's a good firm mattress," you might want to respond, "I don't think there's anything better than a good night's sleep on a quality mattress. Squishy mattresses just don't cut it do they?" You are trying to create an opening with the customer, so you can understand what the customer wants. Once the customer senses that you do understand his interests, he will naturally seek your assistance.

What was your favorite ride at Pirate Island?

4. Be reassuring, not pushy

What you say and how you say it should be in tune with the customer's personality and mood. In other words, don't be too familiar with someone who behaves in a shy or reserved way. And don't push the humor too far with a more outgoing customer. Be sensitive and think in terms of taking steps toward getting to know someone, rather than achieving an instant friendship. This will make the customer feel comfortable— rather than turning him off with too much attention too soon.

Comments such as "That looks very good on you," and "This is a very fine value" will be appreciated, but only if you are being honest and sincere.

Show the customer you will assist him in the style he prefers. Sales associates who hover over customers as they look through merchandise can make customers feel suffocated. Instead of giving excessive attention, show your interest in the customer by making a positive remark about the item he is looking at such as: "That's our top-of-the-line sander you're looking at." This more subtle approach accomplishes three important things, all of which help create a positive impression of you and the store:

- You've complimented the customer's taste.

- You've assured the customer he's the expert.

- You've showed your own knowledge of purchases that are worthwhile.

If you offer to help the customer and he says, "No, thank you," back off. You may be sincerely trying to help. But the customer may feel you are being too aggressive. You want to be sure to give the customer breathing room, a chance to look at merchandise in a relaxed way. However, do not disappear from the sales floor. That customer may not want your help right then and there, but may need it in a moment.

5. Include the entire shopping party

What you've read so far describes a customer who is shopping alone. Often, you will be dealing with a customer who is with friends, a small child, an older relative, or a mate. An equally important part of making a good impression on the customer is to give good service to those who are with her. This can mean offering a comfortable chair to the other person while you review paper work with the customer. Or you might ask the friend if he would like some complimentary coffee or a magazine or newspaper to read while he waits. A customer with a fussy child might look distressed, and you might ease her stress by making a positive comment about the child or offering a toy to amuse the child while you help the customer. Most of all, be sure to show you care about helping in whatever way you can.

Use good judgment! Your involvement may not be welcomed by the "shopping party" in some cases, such as when a parent is scolding a child or when two shoppers disagree on a purchase.

skill practice: observe effective greetings

Directions: One way to learn about the importance of an effective greeting is to visit a store as a customer. While you're there, pay attention to how the sales associate greets you and interacts with you.

Record your impressions by answering the questions in the first column. Then write some ideas in the second column about how you would approach this situation if you were the sales associate.

What Happened/How Did You Feel?	What Would You Do Differently as a Sales Associate?
How soon after you entered the store did a sales associate make contact with you? _____ _____	
How did the sales associate greet you—what did he or she say? _____ _____	
Did the sales associate try to engage you in conversation?_____ If so, how? _____ _____	
What, if anything, did the sales associate say to you to compliment your taste or make you feel like the expert? _____ _____	
What, if anything, did the sales associate say to make you feel confident that he or she understood your needs? _____ _____	
Did you feel comfortable with the sales associate's manner? Why or why not? _____ _____	

Create Customer Loyalty

Your friendly greeting is just the first step in creating a good relationship with a customer. To bring that customer back again and again, you will need to show the customer that your whole job is to serve her. Let's say you helped her locate the perfect toaster (she wanted it to have slots wide enough to toast English muffins or bagels). You also explained what a good warranty it has (two years, not the usual six months). And you reassured her that this has been a reliable and popular product.

> **Ask yourself what you can do to earn the loyalty of your consumers. And, then, deliver. You'll have earned their allegiance for life.**
>
> —Faith Popcorn, trend analyst
> "The Popcorn Report"

Building trust . . . The toaster customer is learning to trust you because you have responded to her needs and given her good information, first steps in building her trust. By listening carefully, you have also picked up hints about how you might help her in the future (perhaps she mentioned she is changing her decor, which influenced her color choice in the toaster.) As you complete this transaction, you will want to tell her that you've enjoyed helping her and would be honored to help her again. If you have a business card, you can offer that to her so she can ask for you by name next time (or you can write your name on the sales slip).

Over time, customers who appreciate your good service will return to you for help in purchasing new items. They may also recommend you and your store to friends and business associates. And they may feel so confident that you understand their tastes and preferences that they will depend on you to act as a personal shopper for them. Now that they know and trust you, they will return the respect you have given them.

45 percent of customers say they are likely to spend more if the sales associate is helpful, according to market research. On the other hand, 18 percent of customers will walk out of a store if they don't like the attitude of the sales associate.

Create Customer Loyalty (cont.)

By this point you can see the power and importance of your work in building customer relations. In the short term, your employer expects you to achieve adequate sales each day. But your employer's first goal is to have loyal customers who return to the store again and again because of the good service they receive.

The true rewards . . . Of course, it is good business to treat customers well. They're more likely to come back for additional purchases. Beyond that, you will achieve personal satisfaction in knowing you've been helpful. Everyone feels rewarded—the store, the customer, and you—when the customer has pleasant memories of her experience long after you complete the sale. You will have your own pleasant memories of having successfully begun a new customer relationship with someone who feels you are a helpful sales associate and a real person.

In Lesson 1 you explored the first steps in creating good relationships with customers. You learned some techniques for greeting customers and beginning the process of creating customer loyalty.

In Lesson 2 you will discover how much you can learn about customers by simply observing their actions soon after they enter your store.

LESSON 2

Build Relationships, One Step at a Time

Now that you understand how important customer service is to the ongoing success of a retail business, you'll learn how you can improve your ability to deliver the highest quality service in a variety of circumstances. No single book can cover every possible situation or type of customer. But the tools that follow are designed to help you build customer relationships that will last.

You'll learn how to discover as much as you can about your customers and their needs. And you'll begin to use proven techniques for gathering and using client information to increase sales opportunities.

As you put these tools and techniques to work, you'll gain confidence in your ability to serve each new customer, no matter how challenging. Being prepared to offer a tailor-made solution begins with getting to know your customers. As with other relationships, this involves a progression of steps and actions that build on each other. These steps should include the following:

- **Be observant**
- **Determine a customer's needs**
- **Keep the lines of communication open**
- **Fit the products to the customer**
- **Offer alternatives**
- **Know when to refer a customer elsewhere**

Be Observant

Getting to know a customer begins with your first encounter. How customers respond to your greeting may tell you if they are in a hurry, have a specific need, or have other priorities. You can learn a lot about a customer by simply watching for a moment; if he walks directly to a certain item without looking at other things along the way, this customer probably knows exactly what he wants and would appreciate quick, efficient service. If, on the other hand, a customer seems to be browsing happily, your best approach will be to greet him, offer to serve him as soon as he is ready, and give him some space to browse.

Other clues include:

- **Constantly checking price tags.** You might want to make sure this customer is aware of any specials your store is having by mentioning, "All frames are 25 percent off this week."

- **Scanning the area, looking above the merchandise rather than directly at it.** You should check if the person needs directions by saying, "You seem to be looking for something—or someone—can I help you with directions?"

- **Looking around for the store clock.** You might say "If you are in a hurry, I'd be happy to help you find something."

- **Difficulty deciding between similar items.** You can ask questions that will help you understand why the customer can't decide; then offer additional information that would be helpful such as "We have matching accessories for that line of sheets but not the other."

Be Observant (cont.)

When a customer focuses in on specific items, engage him in conversation that will help you learn more about his interest in that item. As a customer service professional, you will want to keep track of those important first impressions. This will help you improve your understanding of that customer as you learn more about him. A written record of vital information about your regular customers—or people you want to cultivate as regular customers—can be one of your most important working tools. You will learn more about creating a client record at the end of this section.

Practice being observant and providing the right response to customer clues by playing the detective game on the next page.

skill practice: you be the detective

Directions: Before you simply ask "Can I help you?" observe customers' actions for clues to their needs and desires. Practice this by playing detective with these clues.

Pick a response from below that might help you get more than a "No, I'm just looking" comment from the customer. Write the letter for the response next to the customer clue. We've done the first one for you.

CUSTOMER CLUE

The customer is picking up every object on one particular display, seemingly comparing the items to each other.   **B**

A man is casually browsing and picking up items that might be for a woman.   _____

The customer heads straight for one display, looks briefly and then begins to leave the store.   _____

The customer keeps picking up and then putting down the same item, seemingly unable to make a decision.   _____

The customer walks in with a shopping bag from your store, goes directly to a particular display and begins searching for something.   _____

The customer gets a shopping cart, pulls out a shopping list and begins going up and down each aisle slowly.   _____

SALES ASSOCIATE RESPONSES

A. Say "I'm sorry you didn't find what you were looking for…perhaps I can help?"

B. Comment "We just got those in — aren't they lovely?"

C. Say "Can I help you with a return or exchange?"

D. Comment "Looks like you are considering a gift—is there a special occasion?"

E. Comment "Let me know if you need help finding anything."

F. Say "You seem undecided…have you used that product before?"

Compare your answers to those in the back of the book.

Notes:

Now that you've completed Lesson 2 and taken a turn at being the detective, compare your responses on page 31 to those in the back of this book. You can learn a great deal about customers by observing their actions. This will provide clues on how to best approach them and offer further assistance.

Lesson 3 will help you take the next step in determining customer needs—knowing what questions to ask.

LESSON 3

Determine a Customer's Needs

When a person walks into a store, she enters with a desire—conscious or subconscious—to purchase what that store is selling. Shoppers want to buy. Your job as a sales associate is to ensure that customers' needs are satisfied—to help them complete the buying process. Once you've established a friendly connection with a customer, your next challenge is to determine exactly what the customer needs—both goods and services. Many customers know exactly what they want. Others may have only a general idea. Some have nothing specific in mind, only the hope of finding something that will satisfy their desire to buy. The ultimate goal for you is the same for all these cases: to satisfy the customer.

Even if you are assisting a very independent shopper who has already found exactly what he was looking for, you can make a positive impression by taking care of unspoken needs. For example, you can ring up the sale promptly. You may also be able to provide product care advice, warranty information, a product booklet, directions to the next department the customer is looking for, etc. But mostly, these customers will appreciate immediate attention and efficient service.

You can become skillful at anticipating customer needs by gathering information about the customer in two ways: first, through careful observation; and second, by asking thoughtful questions.

Knowing the questions to ask . . . Customers may tell you what they want, but they will not always tell you why. If you ask the right questions, you can find out their buying motive, and thus improve your chances of satisfying customers and making sales. Ask searching questions to determine what the customer likes and needs. Then use your imagination. The customer searching for a baby gift may not know what types of gifts are appropriate. You can ask questions about the baby—age, whether it's a boy or girl, if it's a first-born, etc.—and then make helpful suggestions about clothing, nursery furnishings, books, or toys.

The customer looking for a VCR may be attracted by such features as ease of use or low price. Help the customer come to a decision by "tuning in" to help the customer narrow his focus. Most importantly, ask questions that encourage conversation. Questions beginning with *who, what, where, when, how,* and *why* will open doors. *Yes/no* questions are liable to close them.

Questions that open doors

- *Who* are you shopping for?
- *Who* told you about our store?
- *What* brings you into the store today?
- *What* is the special occasion?
- *Where* have you seen one before?
- *Where* will it be used?
- *When* is the special occasion?
- *When* did you decide that you had to have one?
- *How* did you hear about us?
- *How* long have you been shopping for one?
- *Why* that specific model or brand?

skill practice: opening doors with open-ended questions

Directions: The best way to get customers talking is to ask *open-ended questions*.

When you ask customers *yes* or *no* questions, you don't get the whole story. You might learn *what* the customers want or don't want, but they do not reveal *why*. Open-ended questions invite customers to "tell more," which will help you learn more about their needs.

Compare the examples of dead-end and open-ended questions. Then turn the last few examples of dead-end questions into open-ended questions.

Compare your answers to the suggestions in the back of the book.

DEAD-END	OPEN-ENDED
• Can I help you?	• How can I help you?
• Do you like red or green?	• What color do you prefer?
• Is that the brand you want?	• Why do you prefer that brand?
• Is this for you, or is it a gift?	• For whom are you shopping?
• Did you want a full skirt?	• Which style skirt did you want?
• Do you want preset controls?	• What features are important to you?
• Is it for a special occasion?	• What's the special occasion?
• Looking for anything special?	• What are you looking for?
• Did you see our coupon specials?	• _____
• Do you like 100 percent cotton?	• _____
• Do you prefer do-it-yourself assembly?	• _____
• Is this all for you today?	• _____
• Have you read this author before?	• _____

After completing Lesson 3, compare your answers from page 36 to the suggestions in the back of this book.

Now that you've learned how to ask open-ended questions, Lesson 4 will help you keep the lines of communication open by avoiding dead-end responses like "no thanks, just looking."

LESSON 4

Keep the Lines of Communication Open

Knowing the questions NOT to ask . . . Certain questions not only lead to deadends, they can poison a sale. Avoid directly asking the customer how much she wants to spend. Of course there are some situations where you need to know the customer's price range so you don't waste her time by showing her things she doesn't want. But approach this issue in an open-ended manner so you don't eliminate possibilities she might not have considered. Ask questions about the quality she is interested in, her reasons for purchasing, etc. Asking "What clothing lines do you usually prefer?" or "What kind of refrigerator do you currently have?" will give you clues about her price range.

Also, avoid either/or questions that force customers to choose options before they have reviewed them. Rather than simply saying "We carry three styles of that lamp...which one do you want?" help customers compare their needs to product features. "Here are the three most popular styles of that lamp and each provides a different kind of light...what kind of lighting effect are you looking for?"

When asking why questions, be careful not to put the customer on the defensive. Rather than asking "Why do you like the Northern refrigerator?" say something like "We sell a lot of those refrigerators...what qualities of the Northern do you like?"

After you've asked, listen . . . If customers feel that you listen, understand, and care about what they say, they will trust you. If they trust you, they are more likely to buy from you. As you question your customer in the open-ended style we've described, listen actively and interestedly to what the customer says in response. Show your interest with a statement that says, "I know where you're coming from." Customers appreciate a sales associate who shows understanding and is interested in their needs, not just in making a sale.

Step by step . . . Each response to the questions you ask should lead toward knowing better how you can meet this customer's needs. Your skill in getting good feedback—from the purpose of the customer's purchase down to the details on price, brand, color, size, etc.—will help you succeed in two ways: (1) meeting the customer's current need, and (2) showing the customer that you can meet his future needs.

skill practice: encouraging conversation

Directions: As a sales associate, you must do more than just make contact with customers, you must also engage them.

Read the customer statements and then write a response that will encourage further conversation.

CUSTOMER	SALES ASSOCIATE
1. "I was hoping you had some new items for my collection."	_____
2. "I'm looking for a hair dryer."	_____
3. "I need a birthday present for a co-worker."	_____
4. "I'm just looking, thanks."	_____
5. "I need a better tennis racket."	_____
6. "I need a new shirt."	_____
7. "Where is the perfume department?"	_____

Compare your answers to the suggestions in the back of the book.

Of course, how you, as an individual, encourage conversation will depend on your own personality and that of your customers. Compare your responses on page 40 to the suggestions in the back of this book for some additional ideas on how to keep the lines of communication open.

The next step in building customer relations is especially important. Lesson 5 will help you fit the right products to the customer. And remember—this will all get easier with practice!

LESSON 5

Fit the Products to the Customer

Finding the right fit, regardless of the product or service involved, is essential to customer satisfaction. A person shopping for new appliances for an apartment may need a stackable washer and dryer rather than a full-sized side-by-side set. A parent looking for jeans for a child may prefer a slightly oversized fit to allow room for growth. The gardener shopping for shrubs will need to consider height, rate of growth, and hardiness. Your job is to ask questions to help define the right "fit" and then provide options that will meet those needs.

Sometimes fit can be a sensitive issue. If you are selling clothing or shoes, you eventually have to ask "What size?" This is a very personal matter. Never react in a judging way and never contradict the customer. If the customer is uncomfortable giving you a direct answer, think of alternative ways to help.

A Gracious Approach

Pat McCarthy, the legendary menswear sales associate for Nordstrom, describes how he approaches the issue of "fit" in the national bestseller, *The Nordstrom Way*:

"I'll suggest we try on a coat to make sure we have the right size. By doing that we begin to bond. Bonding is essential."

Because McCarthy is six-foot-six inches tall, he takes special care to identify with the customer. If a customer happens to be shorter in stature than average, McCarthy will counter with the flip side of the dilemma: "I bet I have fewer suits in my size than in yours."

In essence, McCarthy is telling the customer that "he's not an oddball...the important thing is that we have established a connection." Throughout the process, McCarthy casually interviews the customer because the "more information you have, the better you can work. What kind of business is he in? What kind of clothes does he wear for business?"

Take your cues from the customer . . . Often, it's best to let the customer volunteer size information. Ask her first if she would like you to bring her items to try on. If she answers "Yes," ask what sizes she would like to try. You could even suggest that the sizes vary between brands and offer to bring several sizes. Give her information that will help her narrow her search. For example, let her know that a brand she has selected runs small, long, or wide, and offer to show her brands, styles, or sizes that might fit her needs.

If a very large man is looking at a chair that may be too small to support him, would you rush and grab it to stop him from sitting in it? Of course not. But you could ask questions that would help you better understand his needs: Is he looking for himself or for someone else? Will the chair be used daily or only occasionally? What is the decorating style of the home? What you learn will help you suggest some models that suit his specific needs, including durability if the chair is for him.

Service extras...Fitting a customer with merchandise just right for his needs may take more than just getting the customer to consider a different size. Some customers may need special-order merchandise, customizing, alterations, or accessories to suit their particular situations. The gardener with acres of lawn may want to order an extra-large grass catcher for his mower. A smaller than average person may need the sleeves shortened on a new jacket. A customer buying a new stove and venting hood may need an adapter for the existing ducting. A new truck owner may need rubber floor mats instead of carpet. If you take time to understand your customers, you can make suggestions to enhance their selections. However, don't assume you know what they want—ask questions. The new truck owner may be using his "rig" to commute to an office, not a construction site! Ask questions and mention any additional services you can provide to help meet your customer's needs. Then let the customer tell you what he needs. Here's when it will really pay off to be a good listener.

skill practice: sizing up your customer

Directions: You can handle "size" issues better if you prepare in advance. Think about how you would handle some possible situations. Review the situations and suggestions on this page.

Then try writing your own script for the situations on the next page. Your suggestions should be based on your own shopping experiences or your work with customers. Just be sure that you include questions that will help "size up" the customer's needs.

Situation 1: A customer is searching for panty hose and you want to help her select the right size. Since panty hose is sized according to height and weight, it would be insensitive to simply ask "How much do you weigh?"

Instead, you might say: "Have you worn this brand before?" If she says yes, ask "What size was most comfortable for you?" However, if she says no, suggest "Let's look at the size chart—where do you see yourself according to their recommendations?"

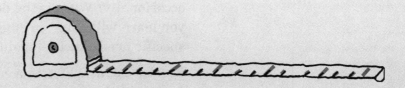

Situation 2: An elderly woman is looking for comfortable shoes. In addition to proper fit, you want to be sure that she selects shoes that she can put on easily and ones that provide good balance.

You might say: "Will you be walking a great deal in these shoes?" "Do you prefer shoes that slip on, lace up, or that have Velcro closures?" "What brands have worked well for you in the past?" "What kind of stockings will you be wearing with your shoes?" "Will you be wearing these mostly on carpeting or on slicker surfaces such as hardwood?"

Situation 3: A middle-aged man is looking for new seat covers for his 20-year-old car. Your store carries inexpensive vinyl seat covers, expensive sheepskin covers, and several options in between, but you don't know what he has in mind. In fact, you don't know if he is the proud owner of a "classic" or just trying to keep his old "clunker" going.

You might say:

_____

_____

_____

_____

_____

_____

_____

_____

Situation 4: A customer is looking for Italian sausage in your specialty foods store. She does not yet have any other items in her grocery basket, so you can't guess what she is planning to prepare or whether she is shopping for a simple family dinner or a dinner party with lots of guests.

You might say:

_____

_____

_____

_____

_____

_____

_____

_____

Compare your answers to the suggestions in the back of the book.

Notes:

There are probably many different ways to size up the customers described on page 45 of Lesson 5. See how your ideas compare to those in the back of this book. This too, is a skill that improves with practice.

Lesson 6 (the final lesson in this section) explores what to do when you can't exactly meet the immediate needs of your customer. This is where being a creative problem solver can really help you achieve customer loyalty!

LESSON 6

Offer Alternatives

Consider how you can serve a customer when your store doesn't have exactly what your customer has requested: Can you offer a different color? A comparable brand? Another model? Often, by knowing both your customer and your merchandise well, you can suggest good alternatives. First, get permission from the customer by asking questions such as: "Could I suggest another possibility?" "Would you consider a comparable substitute?" "Are you set on that particular brand?"

> *Sales Associate:*   *"May I bring some other options for you to try on?"*
>
> *Customer:*   *"I guess, but I really want a rainproof jacket."*

After the customer agrees . . . Okay. So the permission you got from the customer wasn't as enthusiastic as you would like. But you did get a go-ahead, and you're pretty sure you can come up with a great new choice or two. In the best case, your customer likes what you show him. Worst case, he feels you've tried your best to satisfy him. After all, you asked for and got permission to show him other jackets.

When suggesting alternatives, be sure to match the features of the substitute with the customer's interests. In other words, offer an attractive alternative. Don't spoil the customer's experience by continuing to push alternatives on him or insisting that he won't find anything better elsewhere. Hard sells leave bad feelings.

Know When to Refer a Customer Elsewhere

If your store does not offer the particular product or service that the customer is looking for, your first option is always to suggest alternatives. If, however, you are not able to find a suitable alternative, your next options are either to special-order the item for him (of course, only if that's possible at your store), or refer him to a competitor that does carry the item. One further step you can take is to offer to call the competition to make sure they carry the item; then, if they do, give your customer directions to that store. Your thoughtful referral can easily lead to this customer returning to you the next time he needs a product.

When it comes to service . . . If you work in a large store and a customer requests a service that is not available in your department, tell him where he can go for help. Offer to call ahead to the department to tell the sales person there about the customer's needs. Give the customer clear directions on how to get to the department. Better yet, escort the customer to the department if possible (if you're the only associate on duty in your department, you probably won't be free to go this extra step). Your courtesy will impress the customer, and may convince him that you are the sales associate to turn to with a future need.

skill practice: case studies

Directions: Read the stories which follow and decide what the best approach would be to meeting these customers' needs. Use a check mark (✓) to select the solution you think would be best for building customer relations in each case.

CASE 1: THE SOFTWARE SOLUTION

Jacob Waite has decided to do his own income taxes using a popular software program. He has never tried a computer-based tax program, but he read an article about this one and decided it would suit his needs. He goes to Cyber City on Saturday morning to buy the program so he can complete the task over the weekend. Taxes must be mailed by the following Monday at midnight. You are the sales associate trying to help Jacob, but you discover that you do not have this program in stock—it has been a big seller this month. You check with the buyer and find out a new supply is expected any time—in fact, it was expected yesterday. What can you do to help Jacob now?

❑ Tell Jacob you will call him as soon as the new shipment arrives and put one on hold for him. Who knows, it might even come in later today!

❑ Ask Jacob what he read in the article that made this program seem ideal for him. Find out more about what he is looking for and see if you have another program in stock that would fit his needs. If not, call the competition.

❑ Call the competition—this man is in a panic and must have that program pronto!

CASE 2: THE BURNER ISSUE

Heidi Metcalf is looking for a new burner for her gas barbeque. Your store does not stock these, but you can get them in about a week by special ordering from the manufacturer. There is a store about 10 miles away that specializes in barbeque repairs and accessories, and it is likely that they would have the part in stock. Heidi already has a number of items in her shopping cart that look like she is getting ready for spring, although the good weather is still a few weeks away. She is buying some flower seeds, potting soil, a gallon of paint and a few brushes, and a new garden hose. How should you respond to her question about the barbeque?

- ❏ Tell her that the competitor's store may have it in stock, but that she can special order it if she is not in a hurry.

- ❏ Tell her you don't stock that part and refer her to the competitor's store.

- ❏ Tell her that you would be happy to special order the part for her and it will arrive in about a week. Then ask if that is soon enough. If she says yes, proceed with the special order.

Compare your answers to those in the back of the book.

Notes:

When you have practiced meeting customer needs by doing the case study exercises in Lesson 6, compare your answers on pages 50 - 51 to those in the back of this book.

You are almost finished with Part 1. Just complete the Roundup on the next page—you'll see how much you have learned already!

ROUNDUP

Roundup: Get to Know Your Customer

The list that follows is a brief roundup of the customer service concepts you have explored in Part 1. Check (✓) the items which you now feel more prepared to do as a sales associate:

- ❑ Greet customers in a winning way.

- ❑ Observe customers to learn more about their interests and needs.

- ❑ Ask questions that open doors and help you learn more about your customers' needs.

- ❑ Size up customers to help them find the selections that fit their needs.

- ❑ Suggest alternatives that will still appeal to your customer if you do not have the exact item being sought.

- ❑ Refer a customer to another department or a competitor

If you were not able to check one or more of the items listed above, review the pages related to those topics. Keep in mind that practice makes perfect—use these techniques to build your skills at getting to know customers, and soon you will have clients that seek you out!

Congratulations!

In Part 1 you have learned many ways to discover more about each customer you meet. By building relationships carefully, you help customers gain confidence in you and learn to trust you, so they will return again and again. To learn more techniques for providing personalized customer service, continue on to Part 2, *Meet Your Customers' Needs.*

Notes:

part 2

meet your customers' needs

PURSES
AND
HANDBAGS

Beyond Products: Today's Customers Expect More

Success in retailing has always been based on having the right product in the right place at the right time. And advances in technology have enabled resourceful entrepreneurs and forward-thinking businesses to produce and provide new products with incredible efficiency. Today, consumers can obtain almost everything they need and want without leaving the comfort of their homes. People can order groceries over the phone and have them delivered. They can have tires and windshields replaced without pulling their cars out of the driveway. Avid readers may order books via the Internet and have them delivered to their doorstep the next day.

Instead of creating more leisure time, the "conveniences" of modern electronics seem to only raise expectations for individual productivity. Weekly deadlines have been compressed to a daily rush for the overnight express pickup. And that daily stress is now multiplied many times over during the course of an eight-hour shift by demands for instant information, via fax or e-mail. As people's lives become more and more stressful, two divergent things happen on the retail front. Customers may choose to avoid checkout lines, parking hassles and interaction with less-than-efficient sales associates by turning to catalog, phone or electronic shopping. Or, they become more particular about where they spend what little time they have to shop. These people only go where they know they will receive the best service and the little extras that can turn basic errands into a source of entertainment and pleasure.

As a professional sales associate, you have the power to influence which option customers choose. By providing personalized customer service and an enjoyable shopping experience, you will make people want to get out of their homes, park their cars, hang up the phone and come into your store.

Learning Checklist for Part 2

As you complete Part 2, *Meet Your Customers' Needs,* record your progress on this checklist. This checklist can also be used as a basis for discussion with your instructor, supervisor, or mentor as you complete the skill practices and/or you demonstrate the specific skills in the workplace.

Lessons completed		Date completed
❑ Lesson 7:	Make Shopping an Enjoyable Experience	_____
❑ Lesson 8:	Be Resourceful	_____
❑ Lesson 9:	Inform Customers of Additional Services	_____
❑ Lesson 10:	Accommodate Customers with Disabilities	_____
❑ Lesson 11:	Balance Your Service to In-Store and Phone Customers	_____
❑ Lesson 12:	Build Relationships Over the Phone	_____
❑ Lesson 13:	Make and Keep Commitments to Customers	_____
❑ Lesson 14:	Complete Special Orders	_____
❑ Roundup		_____

Learning Checklist for Part 2 (cont.)

	Skills Demonstrated in the Workplace	Date Demonstrated

❑ Make the shopping experience enjoyable for customers _____

Describe the situation and how you demonstrated this skill:

❑ Inform customer of additional services _____

Describe the situation and how you demonstrated this skill:

❑ Respond to personal needs of shoppers _____

Describe the situation and how you demonstrated this skill:

	Skills Demonstrated in the Workplace	**Date Demonstrated**

❑ Balance responsive phone service with
   in-store service   _____

Describe the situation and how you demonstrated this skill:

❑ Schedule personal appointment with
   shopper; select merchandise in advance   _____

Describe the situation and how you demonstrated this skill:

Learning Checklist for Part 2 (cont.)

Skills Demonstrated in the Workplace	Date Demonstrated
❑ Follow through on commitments made to customers	_____

Describe the situation and how you demonstrated this skill:

❑ Complete special orders	_____

Describe the situation and how you demonstrated this skill:

Meet Your Customers' Needs

As you'll learn in Lesson 7, customers expect a pleasant experience when they enter a store. An enjoyable atmosphere and "super service" are two basics!

LESSON 7

Make Shopping an Enjoyable Experience

An attractive, welcoming retail environment and a friendly, helpful sales associate are the basic ingredients for making a customer's shopping experience enjoyable. Many stores now tailor their environments to provide extras their customers will enjoy. For example, bookstores often have overstuffed chairs and reading lamps to invite browsing book lovers to relax and peruse the merchandise. And stores that specialize in children's games and crafts are likely to have a small table or two with chairs, equipped with lots of crayons and paper to allow children to do what they do best—be creative—while parents shop. While you may not have control over whether your store offers these creature comforts, you can make shopping an enjoyable experience by extending small kindnesses to your customers.

> **"Consumers are statistics. Customers are people."**
>
> —Stanley Marcus, Chairman Emeritus
> Neiman-Marcus, Dallas.

To learn more about the small kindnesses you might offer your customers, play the matching game on the next page.

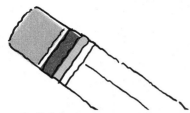

skill practice: the matching game

Directions: Select a "small kindness" that might be welcomed by the customer in each situation. Write the letter of the kindness on the line provided. Hint: one situation has two ideas for small kindness—put both letters on the line next to it. We have done the first one for you.

CUSTOMER SITUATION	LETTER of "MATCHING KINDNESS"
Customer is loaded down with several bags of already-purchased items.	B
Customer buys something that is large, bulky, or heavy.	
Customer is hesitating over a purchase.	
Customer is in no hurry, just wants to browse.	
A customer is accompanied by an elderly person who appears frail or confused; the companion may appear impatient about waiting.	
An elderly customer with limited mobility.	
A person traveling on business or vacation.	
A mother with a fussy infant.	

SMALL KINDNESS

A. Offer to let customer make a local call to verify appropriateness or preference.

B. You can offer to consolidate many small packages into one large shopping bag.

C. Take whatever steps you can to accommodate them immediately, even bending the rules a bit, asking for assistance from a co-worker, or asking another customer to excuse you for a moment while you get this person settled.

D. Let her know if you have a quiet corner or lounge where she can tend to her baby's needs.

E. Offer to temporarily store purchases if customer has more shopping to do.

F. Offer to bring merchandise to the customer while he sits down.

G Offer to deliver the item, carry it to customer's car, or have it available at package pickup.

H. Offer to have packages shipped.

I. Offer a cup of complimentary coffee to make the customer feel welcome.

Compare your answers to those in the back of the book.

Notes:

You are finished with Lesson 7 if you have done all of the reading and completed the skill practice on page 65. Now, compare your responses to the answers provided in the back of this book.

In addition to small kindnesses like these, you can make shopping more enjoyable and convenient for your customers by being aware of other resources in and near your store. Learn more about that in Lesson 8.

LESSON 8

Be Resourceful

To assist your customers in a personal way, you should become familiar with the resources in and near your store. Knowing the answers to the following questions can set you and your store apart.

- Where can a customer have an item gift-wrapped?

- Is there a mailing service nearby? Who sells stamps?

- Where might customers get food or drink, rest their feet, tend to a baby, or wait for a friend?

- Where is the closest pay phone? Can you make change for the phone? Or better yet, does your store allow customers to make free local calls?

- Where is the closest Automatic Teller Machine?

- Is there a credit office in the store? A customer service department?

- Where is the nearest shoe repair shop? Drugstore? Gas station?

- Does your store offer personalizing services, such as monogramming or engraving?

- Is there a tailor or seamstress nearby?

- Does your store offer a gift registry?

- Do any store employees speak other languages?

- Can you offer to enroll the customer in a special rewards program (discounts, rebates, frequent-shopper bonuses)?

- Do you offer free delivery?

- Are there storage lockers or a checkroom for temporary package storage?

- Is there a supervised play area or day nursery in your store or nearby?

- Does your store have a catalog? Can you add your customer to the mailing list?

Sample Resource List

Guido's Grocery customers sometimes ask for—

Table stuff

Table Toppers, Waterfront Market - best source for linens, candles
Big Top Rentals - rents linens, tables, chairs, chafing dishes,
placesettings, etc. (857-0885)
Paper Chase (2 blocks south on 1st) - great invitations, paper napkins

Help for Hire

Catering:
  "Honey I'm Home" specializes in small dinner parties
  (Beth: 442-2237)
  "At Your Service" good for large, corporate parties
  (Jared Perez: 446-1800) also S.C.C. program (see below)
Meal Servers:
  South Community College Hospitality Program, minumum wage. Call
  Program coordinator, Marlene Gregg at 857-9990
Bar tenders:
  Joan Jarvela (from Seahorse Restaurant, 858-3437) - available
  weekends and holidays

Music

  Mambo Magic—Latin (Alex, 340-2323)
  Patti Spring—piano, standards (446-4547)

Cabs

  Blue Sky Cabs: 858-1909

skill practice: create a resource list

Directions: Create a resource list for your customers and keep it handy. You could post it near the cash register, put it in your client book, or attach it to a clipboard for quick reference.

If you are not yet working in a retail store, practice by making a resource list that you, as a customer at your favorite store, would find helpful.

Resource List

_____
_____
_____
_____
_____
_____
_____
_____
_____
_____
_____
_____
_____
_____
_____
_____
_____
_____
_____
_____
_____
_____
_____
_____
_____

As you learned in Lesson 8, being resourceful means being aware of services both in and near your store.

When your store offers service extras such as those described in Lesson 9, you should make a special effort to match those services with customers who will appreciate them. This means paying attention to each customer's unique needs and interests.

LESSON 9

Inform Customers of Additional Services

There are many ways to demonstrate to customers that you and your store appreciate their business. When you take your role as a sales associate seriously, you will find unique ways to show customers you care. One simple way is to make sure they are aware of all the support services your company provides. Depending on the store's policies, such "extras" may include:

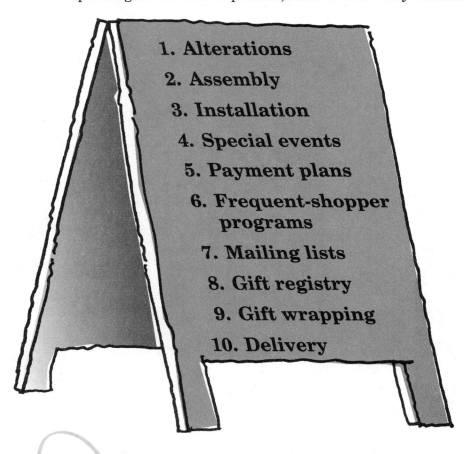

1. Alterations
2. Assembly
3. Installation
4. Special events
5. Payment plans
6. Frequent-shopper programs
7. Mailing lists
8. Gift registry
9. Gift wrapping
10. Delivery

Make a note in your client record system whenever a customer requests any of the service "extras" your store offers. You can use this information to provide more personalized service when those customers return in the future.

1. Alterations

If the customer is interested in alteration or customizing services:

- Explain any fees
- Arrange for the service
- Make sure the altered items meet the customer's needs

2. Assemble and finish

While businesses that sell do-it-yourself products are booming, some people still like to have the job done by a professional. Advertise installation services to your customers, if they are available. If the installation is not included in the purchase price, tell the customer how much it will cost. Some retail shops will also assemble "assembly required" items or finish unfinished furniture for their customers. Many customers are more likely to return to a store that they know offers such product support services.

3. Special events

If the store is holding a special sale or other promotional event in the near future, tell the customer. It gives the customer a reason to return to the store, which means a sales opportunity for you! Such events might include:

- Clearance sales
- Product demonstrations
- Workshops
- Visits by manufacturer representatives

Mentioning specific events that you think customers will benefit from lets them know you and your company really care about meeting their needs.

Inform Customers of Additional Services
(cont.)

4. Ways to pay

Depending upon the size and type of business, some retailers offer special payment options or credit plans. Payment options include:

- Layaway: a deposit holds the item until it is paid in full, usually over the course of a few months.

- In-house accounts: credit cards or credit accounts, sometimes managed by the store itself, rather than a bank. Some retailers offer a discount to customers who open such an account "on the spot." Account holders may also qualify for future "exclusive" discount offers.

- Interest-free credit purchases: some stores offer "same as cash" terms for expensive items, providing the purchase is paid in-full by a specific date. The terms may extend payments anywhere from 3 months to a full year, before any interest fees are added.

5. Frequent shopper programs

Bonus programs for frequent shoppers are a growing trend in retailing. Coffee vendors establish customer loyalty by making the tenth latte free. Some kitchen stores will keep track of your purchases and award a bonus serving piece when you have accumulated eight place settings of dinnerware. Even drugstores have started programs that offer ten percent rebates on money spent over a six-month period. If your store has such a program, be sure to tell your customers about it, carefully explain the terms, and offer to get them started earning bonus awards.

6. Mailing lists

Ask customers if they want to have their name added to the store's mailing list. Mailing list customers often receive special flyers or discount coupons not available to the general public.

7. Gift registry

Many stores offer a gift registration service for people who are approaching a major event. Gift registration may be available for:

- Wedding gifts
- Baby shower gifts
- Housewarming gifts

8. Wrap it up

Many customers are willing to pay for gift wrapping; some stores offer this service for free. When a customer makes a purchase, ask if it is intended as a gift. If so, then either offer to wrap it (if appropriate), or direct the customer to the gift-wrapping desk. Be sure to mention whether the service is free, or there are charges for gift wrapping.

9. Delivery service

Not all purchases are easy to take home. Be sure to tell a customer with a bulky or heavy item if delivery is available. Again, if store delivery service is free, make sure the customer knows. If there is a charge, explain it. Then help make arrangements for delivery if appropriate.

Commonly Offered Service Extras

The following table outlines service extras commonly offered by different types of retailers.

TYPE OF RETAILER	ALTERATIONS/ CUSTOMIZATION	ASSEMBLY	DELIVERY	FREQUENT SHOPPER INCENTIVES	
1. Apparel	tailoring/ monograms		X		
2. Automotive dealers, supplies & services					
3. Book, music, video stores			X	X	
4. Building materials, home improvement	paint, window coverings, etc.	X	X		
5. Catalog stores, mail-order and electronic commerce	X		X	X	
6. Department stores	X	X	X	X	
7. Drug and proprietary stores	prescriptions		X	X	
8. Eating and drinking establishments	X		X	X	
9. Electronics (TV, stereo, computer, etc.)	X		X		
10. Fashion accessories				X	
11. Food stores	cake decorating, meat cutting	deli platters	X		
12. Furniture stores, stoves & outdoor furnishings	upholstery options	X	X		
13. Garden supplies, plants and florists	garden planning	flower arranging	X	X	
14. General merchandise, variety stores					
15. Gift and card shops	imprinting			X	
16. Hobbies/arts, incl. music, craft supplies, fabric stores		garment finishing			
17. Household appliances		X	X		
18. Jewelry stores	sizing, engraving				
19. Home accessories	window coverings	X	X	X	
20. Luggage, leather goods	monograms				
21. Office supplies, software resellers			X		
22. Pet, feed & farm supplies			X	X	
23. Shoe store	stretch, repair, dye				
24. Sporting goods, recreational equipment		X	X		
25. Warehouse clubs	photo finishing				

	GIFT REGISTRY	GIFT WRAPPING	INSTALLATION	MAILING LISTS	PAYMENT OPTIONS	SPECIAL EVENTS
	X	X		X	X	fashion shows
			X		X	
		X		X		author signings/book clubs
			X			workshops
		X		X		
	X	X	X	X	X	vendor demos
			medical equipment	X		
					X	private parties
			X	X	X	
		X		X		ear piercing, scarf tying
						cooking demos
			X	X	X	decorating classes
			planting services	X		workshops
		X				
	X	X		X		
				X		workshops
			X		X	
	X	X		X	X	special showings
	X	X	X		X	decorating classes
				X		
				X	X	
				X		pet care clinics
				X		
				X		workshops
			tile, carpeting			

skill practice: make a list of service extras

Directions: If you are currently working in a retail store, make a list of service extras your company provides. Add to that list service extras that you think your customers would appreciate and share your ideas with your supervisor.

If you are not currently working in a retail position, create a list of service extras that would make shopping more enjoyable and convenient for you. Revisit this list when you begin your retail career and consider which service extras might be important to your new customers.

Service extras available in your store:

_____

_____

_____

_____

_____

_____

_____

_____

_____

_____

_____

_____

_____

Service extras that you'd like to recommend to your supervisor:

_____

_____

_____

_____

_____

_____

_____

_____

_____

_____

While retailers do not have an obligation to provide service extras, like those described in Lesson 9, the smart ones will find ways to make their store more attractive than the competition's.

Smart retailers also recognize the value of making their stores convenient for a significant portion of the population: customers with disabilities. In Lesson 10, we'll explore how you can improve the shopping experience for these customers.

LESSON 10

Accommodate Customers with Disabilities

OBVIOUS DISABILITIES

DISABILITIES THAT YOU CAN'T SEE

Approximately two-thirds of disabilities are not obvious to an observer. We can all see a wheelchair or a cane. However, we cannot see a hearing loss, speech impediment, vision impairment, or brain injury.

By current estimates, 15 to 20 percent of the American population has some type of disability that affects their ability to do day-to-day activities. Therefore, a sales associate should be prepared to encounter a significant disability without warning. The best way to be prepared is to look at this situation from the viewpoint of a person with a disability.

The first thing to realize is that a shopper with disabilities has shopped before and knows what he is doing. He knows what he needs and he recognizes what challenges await him in stores. Most people do not want a great deal of attention to be focused on their disability.

Acknowledge the customer . . . As in building customer relations with anyone, you should make eye contact, smile, and extend an appropriate greeting. Don't interact more with an accompanying able-bodied person than with the shopper with disabilities.

Offering assistance can be tricky. Most people prefer to initiate requests for special assistance themselves. However, a simple, one-time offer such as "If you'd like any assistance, let me know" can be helpful. Never hover, persist, offer judgments, or treat a person with disabilities as a child. Just as in your interactions with all customers, never assume the need for, or attempt to provide, physical assistance unless it has been requested. However, exercise common sense here. You would move boxes out of the aisle for any customer, and doing so to clear the way for a shopper in a wheelchair is obviously the right thing to do. Just don't put the spotlight on customers with disabilities by making a big deal out of it.

Think ahead . . . It would be better not to allow boxes to accumulate in the first place. Anticipate problems your store surroundings might create for customers with disabilities and take steps to accommodate all shoppers. Is the lighting good? Are the aisles wide and uncluttered? Are doors easy to manage? Can a person who is physically-challenged reach products and transport them home? Is there a quiet place for a person to rest and collect his thoughts when the environment becomes noisy and confusing? Are there particular times in the day that the store environment is better for your frequent shoppers who have disabilities—times when the store is less hectic or when there are fewer obstacles to overcome?

Chances are, you may identify some potential problems that you do not have the authority to fix. In this case, be sure to alert your manager to situations which may create difficulties for your customers with disabilities.

Be sincere . . . If you don't understand what the customer is communicating, don't try to fake it. Explain that you're not sure and ask for clarification. The person with disabilities has been through this before and will try to help. If you still don't understand, consider getting a co-worker involved who might be able to understand. Just as we all see the world a little differently, another person may be listening with a different "set of ears."

Accommodate Customers with Disabilities (cont.)

Don't rush . . . Money transactions should never be rushed with any customer. Confirm money transactions, making clear the cost, what the customer has given you, and what the change is. This is good policy with all transactions and can prevent problems later.

And although every disability is different, you can usually predict that working with a customer who has disabilities will probably take a little longer. Trying to speed it up will only make things worse.

In the end, accommodating the needs of people with disabilities is really no different than extending the same courtesies you would to any other customer. Allow customers with disabilities to express their own needs and limits; your job is to accommodate those needs and make shopping a positive experience.

It is better to talk about an "individual," rather than lumping people into a group based on a single characteristic. Rather than referring to someone as "the blind customer," if you don't know her name or must identify her by her disability, you may say, "the customer who is blind." This respects that a person is defined by more than her disability.

Communication considerations for some disabilities

Following are a few common sense suggestions when you are serving customers with obvious disabilities. These are adapted from the book *Americans with Disabilities Act, What You Need to Know*, by Mary B. Dickson.

When communicating with:

- **A person who is hearing-impaired:** Keep in mind that not all individuals who can't hear are able to read lips; many use a combination of techniques including body language and note writing. Even excellent speechreaders will accurately understand about half of what is said. Ask the customer how he would like to communicate, assuming you don't both know how to use sign language.

- **A person who is sight-impaired:** Don't shout unless you know that this person also has a hearing impairment. Speak normally, and don't worry about saying things like "Do you see what I mean?" Most every one uses figures of speech such as this.

- **A person who uses a wheelchair:** When you are having more than a brief conversation, if possible, pull up a chair, sit down, and face this person. How would you like it if you had to look up at people all day!

Accommodate Customers with Disabilities (cont.)

Communication considerations for some disabilities (cont.)

- **A person with developmental disabilities:** Do not talk "baby talk" to this person. However, it may be helpful to explain complex tasks one step at a time. Rather than saying "I'll take this up to the cash register for you and ring it up—do you want to pay with a charge card, cash or a check?" complete one step before you start the next one. For example, wait until you both get to the cash register and then ask one question at a time until you are both clear on the process you will use to complete the transaction.

Just remember, most disabilities will not be as obvious as those mentioned above. Therefore, if you find you are having difficulty communicating with a customer, consider that there may be a disability involved that you are not aware of. Take your time, be patient, and let the customer help you understand what she needs.

> **As one man who uses a wheelchair said, 'I wish people would meet me before they meet my disability'.**
>
> —from Americans with Disabilities Act, What You need to Know
> by Mary B. Dickson

In Lesson 10 you learned that being attentive to customer needs includes being prepared to serve customers with disabilities. Sometimes this is made more difficult by the fact that many disabilities are not obvious.

Being attentive to customer needs can also be challenging when you are helping one customer in the store and another calls on the phone—now what?! Lesson 11 will help you balance your service to both customers.

LESSON 11

Balance Your Service to In-Store and Phone Customers

Not every customer visits the store in person—many will just call on the telephone. These phone-in customers deserve the same quality of service you deliver to customers in person. At the same time, you have to be able to deal with the customer at your counter who wants you to ring up a sale right now! There are several considerations for balancing service between phone customers and those you may already be helping in the store. These include:

1. **Excusing yourself to answer the phone**

2. **Answering the phone politely and professionally**

3. **Putting a customer on hold**

4. **Calling back if necessary**

5. **Being prompt and accurate**

1. Excusing yourself to answer the phone

When the phone rings while you are helping an in-store customer (or a customer on another phone line), excuse yourself politely for a moment. Keep in mind that no customer likes an interruption when she is being served. Besides excusing yourself courteously, reassure the in-store customer that you'll get right back to her. This will help her to be patient while she waits. Then be sure that you *do* get back to her quickly.

2. Answering the phone politely and professionally

Follow these two simple steps to get your relationship with a phone customer off on the right foot: (a) answer the phone promptly, and (b) identify yourself and your department immediately. This way, the customer won't feel like she's been ignored, and she'll know right away that she has (or hasn't) reached the department she wanted.

Always be polite and pleasant, never sound preoccupied or rude. Customer service experts recommend that you actually smile when you answer the phone—your smile will come across in the tone of your voice. Creating a positive first impression will assure the caller that she has made a good choice in calling your store, even if you can't help her right away.

When answering the phone, speak clearly, directly into the mouthpiece, and at a normal pace—never mumble or sound rushed.

Balance Your Service to In-Store and Phone Customers (cont.)

3. Putting a customer on hold

It's good not to routinely place the phone customer on hold. In fact, you should never say "Please hold." Instead, you should ask first and wait for the customer's response. Some folks really have a very simple question that you can answer right away. For example:

Phone Customer: *"What time do you close today?"*

Sales Associate: *"We are open until 5:00 p.m."*

Often you can easily take care of both the in-store customer and the phone customer right on the spot. Then everyone's happy.

However, if the phone customer needs more assistance than the answer to a simple question, you may need to put him on hold or offer to call him back. If you are close to completing a transaction with your in-store customer, it may be acceptable to ask to put the phone customer on hold, especially if the request is urgent.

Phone Customer: *"I'd like to order some flowers to be delivered today."*

Sales Associate: *"We can do that. I'm with another customer at the moment. Could I put you on hold while I finish this transaction—then I can help you with your flower order."*

Phone Customer: *"Okay, I'll hold, if it's not going to be too long."*

Sales Associate: *"Thank you. I'll be right back."*

4. Calling back if necessary

If you anticipate that you will be with your in-store customer a while longer, offer to call back. Your in-store customer will not appreciate feeling rushed if you are helping her with a selection. And pay attention to clues she may be sending you—if she is at all impatient or seems bothered by the interruption, quickly let the phone customer know you are in the middle of a transaction and will call back as soon as possible.

Phone Customer: *"Is your patio furniture still on sale?"*

Sales Associate: *"Yes, but we only have a limited selection left. I'd be happy to call you back in a few minutes and go over our remaining inventory with you if you'd like; I am with another customer at the moment."*

Phone Customer: *"Okay. I'm interested in the metal mesh styles."*

Sales Associate: *"I'll check on those and call you back as soon as I can. What is your name and phone number?"*

Take down the necessary information and repeat back the customer's name and phone number. Don't let your speed in handling this lead to mistakes or make the phone customer feel unappreciated. Close the discussion politely, specifying when he can expect your return call, and then return to your in-store customer and thank her for her patience.

Balance Your Service to In-Store and Phone Customers (cont.)

5. Being prompt and accurate

Make sure to return calls to customers in a timely manner. If you've promised to call back within a specified time, do so even if you don't yet have the answer the customer wants. Let your customer know you are trying to get reliable information and tell him when he can expect to hear from you again.

Sales Associate: *"I have checked on the CD you requested and our system shows that it is available in our warehouse. I expect to be able to confirm that later today and at that time I will get an exact date for when it can be delivered to our store. May I call you back later today with that information?"*

Customer: *"Sure, that would be great."*

Sales Associate: *"Shall I call you back on this number?"*

Customer: *"Yes; if I'm not here just leave a message."*

Keep in mind that a customer who telephones instead of visiting a store is most likely a buyer who knows what he wants. He's probably calling because he doesn't want to waste time traveling to the store to find out about the merchandise price or availability. Therefore, he's depending on you to give him absolutely accurate information.

Phone Customer: *"Do you carry the Tech-no-Buzz Cellular Telephone, and if so, how much is it?"*

Sales Associate: *"Yes, we do carry that model for $199.95. We have three left in stock—would you like me to put one on hold for you?"*

If you tell the customer the item he wants is available and he comes to the store to pick it up, it had better be there—and clearly labeled with his name.

The important thing to remember is that telephone customers have specific needs. How you respond to those needs will determine whether they decide to shop at your store in the future. At the same time, you must show respect and appreciation for the customer who is currently in your store and needing your assistance.

Successful sales associates extend the same high quality service to phone customers as they do to customers already in the store. In this way, they extend their network of loyal customers by making the most of every phone contact.

skill practice: provide balanced service

Directions: For each of the scenarios, decide whether you should respond to the phone request by placing the customer on hold, offering to call the customer back, or helping the customer immediately.

1. You have spent some time greeting a new customer and asking a few questions to get to know her. This customer is being somewhat vague about her needs and seems to just want to look around. Suddenly the phone rings and the phone customer would like some detailed information about a specific item in the store.

   Should you:

   ❑ Offer to call the phone customer back so you can continue asking the in-store customer more questions.

   ❑ Ask to put the phone customer on hold and then go back to the in-store customer to see if she needs any help yet.

   ❑ Help the phone customer now, allowing the in-store customer to browse on her own for awhile.

2. You are in the process of ringing up a sale and there are several other customers waiting in line to pay for their items. The phone rings and the caller says, "I need a gift for my son's birthday dinner tonight. I am really busy today, so I was wondering if you could check whether you have it in stock before I drive all the way down there."

   Should you:

   ❑ Ask to put the caller on hold and check on her request as soon as you are done with your current customer.

   ❑ Explain that you're really busy with other customers at the moment and offer to call her back. This would require stopping what you're doing and writing down her name and phone number.

   ❑ Stop what you're doing and go check on her item immediately, since it won't take long and the phone customer sounds stressed.

3. You are helping a customer who has spent a long time in your department, comparing options and asking you questions about a high-priced item. You are in the middle of reviewing the warranty statement with this customer when the phone rings and someone wants to check on the availability of a sale item advertised in the newspaper.

Should you:

❑ Offer to call back and discuss the sale item as soon as you are done helping the in-store customer.

❑ Ask to put the caller on hold while you check on the sale item, stopping on the way to assure the in-store customer you will be back with him in a moment.

❑ Focus on the phone customer; the in-store customer has already taken up enough of your time!

Compare your answers to those in the back of the book.

Notes:

Compare your answers for the skill practice on pages 92-93 to those in the back of the book.

As you have learned in Lesson 11, balancing your service between in-store customers and those who call on the phone can sometimes be challenging. But using the suggestions from this lesson will help you show both kinds of customers that you care about meeting their needs.

It is very rewarding when that voice on the other end of the line becomes a satisfied customer. Lesson 12 includes tips for turning those phone calls into long-term customer relationships.

LESSON 12

Build Relationships Over the Phone

Once you've made a successful connection with the phone customer—you located the athletic shoes he's been looking for all over town (and they are on sale)—you will want to encourage him to ask for you by name when he comes in to pick them up. This is one more step in establishing a long-term relationship with your customer, and giving the store a personal face.

Some other methods for turning phone callers into loyal customers include:

- **Offering additional information and services**

- **Scheduling in-store appointments**

- **Showing your appreciation**

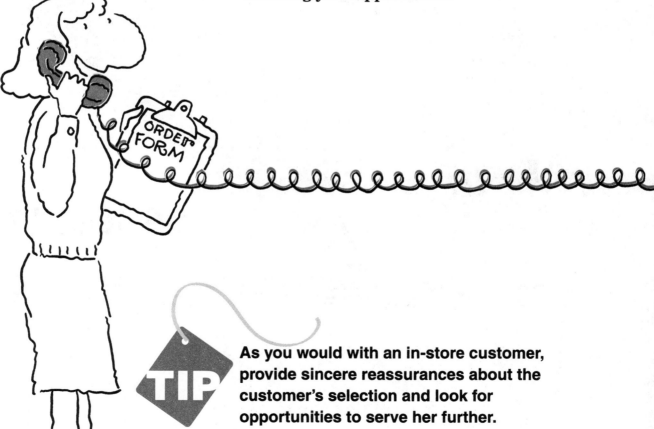

TIP

As you would with an in-store customer, provide sincere reassurances about the customer's selection and look for opportunities to serve her further.

Offering additional information and services

You can turn a telephone inquiry into an ongoing customer relationship by anticipating unspoken needs and offering additional information and services that your customer might appreciate. Such full-service responses might even encourage the customer to seek you out personally in the future. And even if you never meet that customer face-to-face, you can establish yourself as a "can-do" kind of person that the customer can depend on, again and again, because reliable, helpful service is only a phone call away.

When appropriate, suggest additional ways that you can help the caller, perhaps by mentioning services he may not be aware of. If you can, offer to have the requested item shipped directly to the customer. If you do not have the requested item, offer to special order it. Let the phone customer know about sales events or special promotions related to the item he has called about.

Sales Associate: *"I can charge the rug to your credit card and have it delivered to your home if you like. Delivery is free for purchases over $500, so there would be no additional cost to you."*

Customer: *"That would be great. Here's my account number..."*

Sales Associate: *"Okay, looks like you're all set. I've enjoyed working with you and I'm sure you're going to love that rug. But if it doesn't work out, or you have any questions, don't hesitate to call me. And I should let you know — we're having a big sale on lamps and other home accessories next month, so give me a call or come see me if you need anything else to go with that rug."*

Build Relationships Over the Phone (cont.)

Offering additional information and services (cont.)

Just keep in mind, the phone customer is probably trying to save time by calling instead of visiting the store, so don't prolong the conversation—just let him know you have his interests in mind. If your phone customer emphasizes that he only wants to know one thing, the most "sales-worthy" thing you can do is answer his question promptly, precisely and politely.

Customer:	*"Do you carry Kids Kraft Kits?"*
Sales Associate:	*"Yes we do; what model are you looking for?"*
Customer:	*"I just wanted to know if you carry them before I bring my daughter in. Thank you."*
Sales Associate:	*"You're welcome, and thank you for calling; we look forward to serving you and your daughter. When you come in, please look for me — my name is . . ."*

The important thing is to give the phone customer the information he wants and needs, showing him that calling you was the right decision. That way he'll call you first when he needs something in the future.

At the end of this lesson, you'll have a chance to practice developing full-service responses to questions asked by phone customers.

Scheduling in-store appointments

If your phone customer isn't exactly sure about what she wants (perhaps she called to check prices, but doesn't have a specific model in mind), you can suggest scheduling an appointment to help her make a selection. She can give you a few guidelines—like size, price range, features, etc.—and you can be prepared to spend some time helping her decide.

> **Customer:** *"How much do you charge for golf clubs—I've just signed up for lessons, but I don't want to spend too much until I know if I'm going to like this sport."*
>
> **Sales Associate:** *"They really range, depending on what you're looking for. Since you're new to the sport, perhaps I can take some of the mystery out of buying golf clubs. If you'd like to come in at a certain time, I will make sure I'm here to explain what you should look for and help you pick a set that is best suited to you."*
>
> **Customer:** *"That would be great. As long as you realize I may want to shop around before I make a final decision."*
>
> **Sales Associate:** *"Absolutely! In fact, I encourage you to, because I know our prices are competitive. Besides, I love helping people get started in this sport. When would be the best date and time for you? We're open 7 days a week, 9 to 5."*

If the customer cannot come into the store, but would like some additional one-on-one help from you, be creative in offering solutions. If she needs more information about a product, offer to send or fax product literature to her. Offer to put her on the mailing list for catalogs, sales notification, etc. Ask if she'd like for you to research an item and call her back. The point is to find ways that you can serve your phone customers further to meet their needs and build long-term relationships.

Build Relationships Over the Phone (cont.)

Show your appreciation

As you would with an in-store customer, always thank phone customers for calling, even if they don't buy anything. When the call does result in a sale, thank the customer for his purchase, order, or whatever transaction occurs, and invite him to ask for you by name next time he is in the store. If you are shipping a purchase to the customer, consider enclosing a handwritten note thanking the phone customer for doing business with your store; include your name and extension number. If you have a business card, enclose that as well.

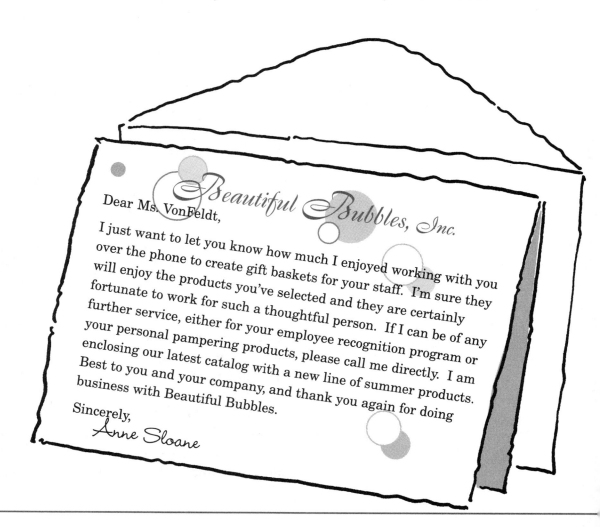

Dear Ms. VonFeldt,

I just want to let you know how much I enjoyed working with you over the phone to create gift baskets for your staff. I'm sure they will enjoy the products you've selected and they are certainly fortunate to work for such a thoughtful person. If I can be of any further service, either for your employee recognition program or your personal pampering products, please call me directly. I am enclosing our latest catalog with a new line of summer products. Best to you and your company, and thank you again for doing business with Beautiful Bubbles.

Sincerely,
Anne Sloane

skill practice: full-service responses

Directions: Telephone customers present a great opportunity to build customer relations. By giving them the same service you would offer to your in-store customers, you invite them to call on you again.

Review the following examples and then write some of your own full-service responses.

Compare your answers to the suggestions in the back of the book.

PHONE CUSTOMER

How late are you open tonight?

Do you carry the Homestead Collectibles?

I'm looking for Waffle Walkers in size 8.

Can you tell me if my prescription is ready?

What is your price on the Reliable Baby Monitor?

How long do custom orders take?

Do your bicycles come already assembled?

SALES ASSOCIATE

Thanks for calling—we're open until 5:00 tonight, which is only another 30 minutes. Can I help you find something while we're on the phone?

Yes we do. Is there a particular one you are looking for? They sell out rather quickly, so I'd be happy to put one on hold for you if you'd like.

That is one of our most popular shoes. If I may put you on hold for moment, I'll check to see if we have size 8 in stock. By the way, do you have a color preference? They come in black, brown, and tan.

_____
_____
_____
_____

_____
_____
_____
_____
_____

_____
_____
_____
_____

_____
_____
_____
_____

Notes:

The full-service responses you developed on page 101 for Lesson 12 will probably depend on your own personality and experience, but compare yours to the suggestions in the back of this book.

In Lesson 13 you will learn that in making commitments to customers, it is important to say what you'll do and do what you say.

LESSON 13

Make and Keep Commitments to Customers

Nothing reassures a customer more than a sales associate following through on her promises. Remember, you represent the store and its values and service. To that customer, you *are* the store.

- When you promise to call a customer back, do so.

- When you offer to check on merchandise availability, be prompt and accurate.

- Fill orders on time.

- Follow up on special orders. Prove to customers that they can count on you.

Keeping commitments to customers may sometimes require you to make an extra effort. But that extra effort will pay off by building customer loyalty.

> **" In the best institutions, promises are kept no matter what the cost in agony and overtime. "**
>
> —David Ogilvie, advertising specialist

Say what you'll do . . . When you make commitments to customers, be very clear on what you are promising. Conclude your discussion by reviewing the steps you will take and what the customer can expect as a result. Make notes, if necessary, so you will remember what you have promised.

For example, you can help customers locate out-of-stock items by promising to call your distribution center, warehouse, or associated stores if your company is part of a chain. You can promise to have the item transferred to your store, or even sent directly to the customer if appropriate for your business. Then:

1. Ask the customer how he would like to be notified

2. Take down the necessary information

3. Specify when he should expect to hear from you

A word of caution here: *Never make promises you can't keep.* For example, if Mr. Jones wants a specific model of wheelbarrow, you may promise to find out if it is on back order or available from another outlet. But don't promise you will find it unless you are positive you can. Most people are happy to know you will do your best and don't expect miracles. Make only promises that you can keep, and then keep them!

And do what you say . . . Even if you haven't yet located that wheelbarrow, contact Mr. Jones by the agreed time to let him know you're still trying. Checking in with him when you said you would demonstrates that:

- You are considerate

- You care about helping him

- You are reliable

Keeping him informed of your progress may also prevent him from looking elsewhere, giving you an opportunity to meet his needs and keep him as a customer. If, after your best efforts, you cannot locate that wheelbarrow, you may suggest a reasonable alternative. If your store does not have a suitable substitute, you can still provide quality customer service by letting Mr. Jones know if the wheelbarrow he wants is available at a competitor's store. This way you have kept your promise and met his needs, two essential steps in building customer relations.

If, in spite of your good intentions, you find you are not able to keep a promise you have made, always call the customer and tell him. When store policy or internal issues prevent you from keeping a commitment, let the customer know. Be sure to apologize for any inconvenience this may have caused him.

Make and Keep Commitments to Customers (cont.)

Explain what you can't do . . . The rules your company has created will guide you in providing fair and equal treatment to every customer you serve. If a customer asks you to do something that is against company policy, explain why you cannot. Most people understand and appreciate rules that:

- Prevent you from making promises you can't keep

- Preclude customer disappointment

- Protect customers and employees from danger

- Provide the company reasonable and fair financial protection

Making exceptions . . . However, things may not always be so clear-cut. For instance, you may work for a company that encourages its sales associates to push the limits of the company rules, if necessary, in order to serve a customer. In such a case, you might have the authority to make exceptions to the rules. For example:

Sales Associate: *"We don't normally allow our customers to take jewelry from the case and walk around the store wearing it. But I know how important it is for you to see how the necklace will look with the dress you're considering. I'll ask our fashion consultant to escort you to the designer dresses, and she'll return the jewelry when you're done."*

By making it clear that you are making an exception, you help the customer understand that this not a standard practice. That way she won't unknowingly break such rules in the future—she'll check with a sales associate first. This protects the customer. You are also letting her know that you value her as a customer and are willing to take special measures to meet her needs.

skill practice: keeping commitments

Directions: To make sure you can meet your commitments to customers, you will need to plan ahead. Sometimes, you will also need to ask your co-workers to help you.

Here are some examples of when planning and teamwork would be helpful. Add some of your own ideas or experiences.

PLANNING: When you need to plan ahead . . .

- Planned absences—vacation, days off, doctor appointments, daycare duty, etc.

- Times when your store is especially busy—special sale events, holiday shopping, etc.

- Allowing time to unpack and distribute an item that has a long list of customers waiting for it.

- Other situations that require planning ahead:

_____

_____

_____

_____

_____

TEAMWORK: When you need to ask for help . . .

- If your special customer arrives to pick up an item you have on hold for him, but you are in the middle of helping another customer.

- When you need special expertise (example: you're not sure which motor oil is best for your customer's car).

- If the customer is in a hurry, you can team-up to get the order rung up, packaged, and out the door more quickly.

- Other situations that call for team work:

_____

_____

_____

_____

_____

Notes:

Planning ahead and working as a team will help you keep the commitments that you make to customers. The list of ideas you've started in Lesson 13 will grow along with your experience in working with customers.

Keeping commitments is a skill you will also use when you help a customer with a special order. In Lesson 14 you will learn that becoming an expert at special orders can add interest and opportunity to your work as a sales associate.

LESSON 14

Complete Special Orders

Helping a customer with a special order can sometimes make or break a customer's loyalty to a store. Many book buyers, for example, will only shop at bookstores where salespeople will special-order books that are out of stock (or that have just been published and are due to arrive soon). People are busy and appreciate not having to track down merchandise themselves. The more you help a customer with "one-stop shopping," the more you can count on him to return to you for future purchases.

Make special your specialty . . . Special orders should not be considered an added burden, extra work, or a thing to dread. Sale associates should view special orders as an opportunity to provide additional service and build customer loyalty. In fact, in many retail situations, special orders are a routine part of the business. If you look for opportunities to serve your customers through special ordering, you will not only gain their loyalty, you'll develop greater product knowledge and increase your ability to serve future customers with special needs.

Be prepared . . . If you do not normally deal directly with vendors, find out who does. This is your resource for answering customers' special requests. Large retailers often have specialized buyers.

Keep records of any correspondence between you and your customers or vendors. Records of all special orders should be carefully organized and accessible to co-workers in case you are not available to complete the transaction.

If your company expects you to take care of special orders yourself, make sure you know where product books (other literature provided by manufacturers) are located. When you're not busy helping customers, take a few minutes to look through this information and become familiar with product options that your customers may be interested in. There are many benefits to becoming the expert at special ordering! Before you're faced with a special-order situation, prepare yourself by running through the steps of the special order process so that you are prepared with:

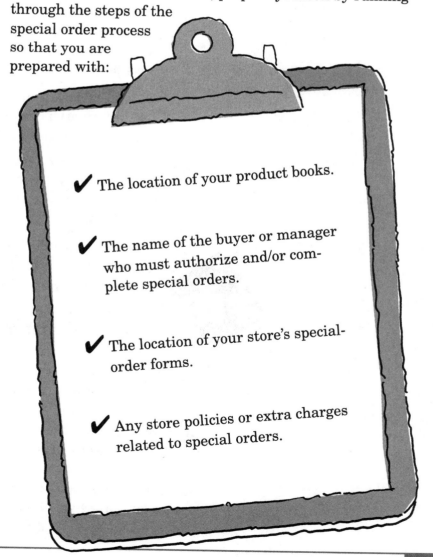

✔ The location of your product books.

✔ The name of the buyer or manager who must authorize and/or complete special orders.

✔ The location of your store's special-order forms.

✔ Any store policies or extra charges related to special orders.

Complete Special Orders (cont.)

The benefits of being a special order expert

Here are a few good reasons for considering special orders an opportunity, rather than extra work. Check (✓) those that are important to you:

- ❏ Customers will seek you out as their favorite problem-solver (and perhaps the boss will notice!)

- ❏ Processing special orders breaks up the routine of daily activities, adding interest and challenge to your job.

- ❏ You will become more expert on the products your company sells, because you know about options and have learned about the manufacturer.

- ❏ You develop awareness of customer needs and can pass that information to others in the company, such as the department or store manager and buyers.

- ❏ When permitted, interacting with other departments (such as buyers and shipping) and other companies (manufacturers or vendors) may lead to job growth and opportunity.

Make a note on your calendar when special orders are due to be fulfilled. This will re-mind you to check in with the right people in your company and with customers to make sure commitments are being kept.

Your best efforts . . . As you respond to a customer's request for a special order, remember not to promise anything you will not be able to deliver. You can always promise that you'll do every-thing you can to locate the item the customer wants (unless, of course, you already know it's impossible). And you can promise you will give the customer a timely update on your progress. These are things you can control and thus deliver. But you cannot guarantee you'll locate the item itself. This is truly a situation where "A for effort" may be the best you can achieve.

skill practice: processing special orders

Directions: Write up a special order for the following case study, using the form provided. Include all the information necessary to get the order delivered by August 3.

CASE STUDY 2: THE BOOKSHELF BUYER

Rich was responsible for buying bookcases for the new office. He went to Office Organizers and Camille, the sales associate, helped him select bookcases that would fit everyone's needs in the new building. They decided on 10 extra-long pine bookcases, which were not in stock at the store.

The furniture would have to be special ordered, and would be available in about four weeks. Rich requested that the cases be delivered before everyone moved into the new office on August 4th, two weeks from now. Camille explained that there would be an additional fee of $50 for delivery and a $10 rush fee for each of the 10 bookcases. Since the bookcases were oversized, the delivery people would have to use the freight elevator, accessible only by calling Rich first. Rich is in the office between 9:00 a.m. and 5:00 p.m. and his extension is 103.

Customer: Cramer and Associates

Address: 1004 Fifth Avenue

Phone: 445-3808

ITEM	SIZE	QUANTITY	COLOR/FINISH

Deliver to: ☐ Store ☐ Customer Delivery charge: _____

Rush Order: ☐ No ☐ Yes Rush fee, if applicable: _____

SPECIAL INSTRUCTIONS:

Delivery Date: _____

Sales Assoicate: _____

Compare your answers to those in the back of the book.

Notes:

When you have practiced placing a special order by doing the exercise on page 113, compare your completed order form to the one in the back of this book.

You are almost finished with Part 2. Just complete the Roundup on the next page—you'll see how much more you have learned already!

ROUNDUP

Roundup: Meet Your Customers' Needs

In this section, you have learned how a friendly manner and extra efforts build customer loyalty. Each time you behave in a caring way, keep a promise, or follow-up on a special order, you are making a lasting good impression on your customers.

The list that follows is a brief roundup of the customer service concepts you have explored in Part 2.

Check (✓) the items which you now feel more prepared to do as a sales associate:

- ❑ Make a customer's experience enjoyable by offering small kindnesses.

- ❑ Refer customers to resources within and near your store (restrooms, water fountains, nearby cash machines, etc.).

- ❑ Inform customers of additional services offered by your store.

- ❑ Accommodate people with disabilities in a courteous and sensitive way.

- ❑ Provide balanced service between customers in the store and those who call on the telephone.

- ❑ Give full-service responses to telephone customers.

- ❑ Keep commitments to customers, especially by planning ahead and using teamwork.

- ❑ Process special orders and follow up to ensure the customers' needs are met.

If you were not able to check one or more of the items listed above, review the pages related to those topics. In addition, you might consider asking a co-worker, supervisor, friend or family member for advice on how to perform these tasks in a way that would satisfy them if they were your customer. After all, they too shop in retail stores and know how they want to be treated!

Congratulations!

In Part 2 you have discovered how important it is to understand what customers want and need. To learn more techniques for providing personalized customer service, continue on to Part 3, *Build a Continuing Relationship*

Notes:

part 3

build a continuing relationship

Earning Customers' Trust

Personalized customer service begins with greeting customers and getting to know more about them and their needs. It also means making the shopping experience enjoyable by being attentive to their personal needs and offering "service extras." For a truly rewarding career as a professional sales associate, you will want to build long-lasting customer relationships. This kind of customer loyalty is created when customers seek you out personally because they trust you to stand behind the products you sell them and continue to provide excellent service long after the transaction is completed.

You can begin to build that trust before customers leave the store with their new purchases, by making sure they understand product warranties and your store's return policy. Their confidence in you will grow if you handle any complaints as graciously as you do the initial sale. The relationship will be cemented as you follow-up on sales and make sure customers are happy with the products and services you have provided.

Learning Checklist for Part 3

As you complete Part 3, *Build a Continuing Relationship,* record your progress on this checklist. This checklist can also be used as a basis for discussion with your instructor, supervisor, or mentor as you complete the skill practices and/or you demonstrate the specific skills in the workplace.

Lessons completed	Date completed
❑ Lesson 15: Honor Manufacturers' Warranties	_____
❑ Lesson 16: Know Your Company's Return Policy	_____
❑ Lesson 17: Handle Customer Complaints Graciously	_____
❑ Lesson 18: Handle Customer Complaints Graciously (continued)	_____
❑ Lesson 19: Handle Customer Complaints Graciously (continued)	_____
❑ Roundup	_____

Learning Checklist for Part 3 (cont.)

Skills Demonstrated in the Workplace	Date Demonstrated

❑ Honor manufacturers' warranties   _____

Describe the situation and how you demonstrated this skill:

❑ Adhere to company's return policy   _____

Describe the situation and how you demonstrated this skill:

❑ Handle customer complaints   _____

Describe the situation and how you demonstrated this skill:

Build a Continuing Relationship

In Lesson 15 you will learn that you have an important role in helping the customer understand and benefit from product warranties. When something goes wrong or a product does not perform as expected, providing a quick resolution and "service with a smile" will go a long way in helping restore your customers' confidence in you and your store.

LESSON 15

Honor Manufacturers' Warranties

Many name-brand goods carry manufacturer's warranties which protect the customer in the case of damage, defect, or other problems. Some retail companies offer additional "customer satisfaction" guarantees that go beyond the manufacturer's warranty. Some large retailers also offer, for a fee, "extended warranties" or service contracts that cover products beyond the time frame or conditions of a normal warranty.

You are the first point of contact . . . Regardless of the type of warranty, the sales associate is usually the first point of contact when a customer is not satisfied with a product or service. Most customers want face-to-face contact and reassurance that their concerns will be addressed. They don't want to deal with a distant manufacturer, they want to be able to return to the retail store that sold the product.

This provides another opportunity for you to serve the customer well. But it begins with the initial transaction, not when the customer first discovers a problem. As you close a sale, take a few moments to review the terms of the warranty with the customer. These terms are outlined on the Warranty Certificate usually included in the package or on a hanging tag. (See example on page 126.) This document assures the customer that the purchase price will be refunded or the item will be repaired if it fails within a certain period of time. It may even tell the customer where to call for support or service.

According to the text *Retailing Principles and Practices...*

The Magnuson-Moss Warranty Act of 1975 specifically requires that all warranties must be easy to read and understand. A warranty is an agreement that the manufacturer will be responsible for any defects in a product and will replace or repair a product that is faulty. Warranties on consumer products costing more than $10 must be available for consumers to examine before they buy.

The warranty is also an excellent tool for the sales associate to use to reassure the customer about a product's performance, durability, or quality. You should be familiar with the warranties for all products you sell and be prepared to explain them to your customers at the time of their purchase. If you need help understanding the warranty terms, be sure to ask your supervisor. Additionally, you will need to be sure that you have all warranty forms that are required by your company and/or the manufacturer on file and readily available.

Some manufacturers are stricter than others about warranty cards. For example, if you know that a particular manufacturer will not honor a product warranty based only on the customer's store receipt, be sure you tell the customer how very important it is to complete all forms and mail them immediately to the manufacturer.

CUSTOMER SERVICE

Honor Manufacturers' Warranties (cont.)

Here is an example of a product warranty. It is called a "limited warranty," which means it will cover only the exact defects it describes. The warranty is for a baking pan:

Chicago Metallic PROFESSIONAL

Chicago Metallic warrants that each PROFESSIONAL bakeware product is free of defects in material and workmanship. Chicago Metallic will replace FREE any pan that becomes defective during normal use for a period of TWENTY-FIVE YEARS after date of purchase, PROVIDING USER FOLLOWS CARE AND USE INSTRUCTIONS. Return any defective bakeware piece to the address shown below, transportation prepaid.

Use and Care:
- Do not use in microwave ovens
- Dishwasher safe

Return transportation will be prepaid on all merchandise under warranty.

Chicago Metallic PROFESSIONAL
Lander Street
Peoria, IL 53221

How to be an expert . . . If product warranties are especially important to the products you sell, such as appliances, electronics, or tools, you'll probably need to have detailed warranty information readily available. If the company you work for doesn't have a manual that describes all of the major product warranties, create your own. This important tool can be a file or notebook containing copies of product warranties and information for contacting manufacturers.

Things You Can Do As Extra Service

- **Help the customer fill out the warranty card at time of sale, then mail it for him.**

- **Make a follow-up call—check to see that merchandise was delivered on time and in good condition.**

- **Call to see whether there were problems with installation or assembly.**

When a customer returns to you with a product—whether it is protected by warranty or not—you may feel caught in the middle between the company and the customer. You will need to listen carefully and respond in a clear and specific way to the customer, including the upset customer who says to you: "What do you mean it's not covered by the warranty?" You can prepare well in advance for tough questions by knowing your company's policy regarding warranties.

Honor Manufacturers' Warranties (cont.)

Know your company's policy regarding warranties

It is critical that you know your company's standard policy. However, when a customer asks you to make an exception to that policy, you will want to (1) get your immediate supervisor or manager to approve it, and (2) if approved, explain to the customer exactly what you are going to do.

Warranty Questions to Ask Your Manager or Co-Workers

- What, if any, exceptions does your company make to the terms of product warranties?

- Do exceptions to a warranty depend on the type of customer doing the asking—the customer's past history with our organization, the number of previous returns this customer has made, or other factors?

- Who determines when exceptions to the warranty/return policy can be made?

It's very important to give a customer with a warranty problem completely accurate information. Not only does this help the customer, but it firmly establishes your credibility.

Most commonly asked questions about warranties

We've discussed how you can compile your own warranty reference file to prepare yourself for such situations. Your co-workers and supervisor are also a resource to you when you don't have the answer at hand. The following are some of the most common warranty questions you will encounter.

- "Can this item be repaired by the store? If so, will the repair be done in the store or does it have to be sent out? How long will it take?"

- "Does your store have a repair department?"

- "Does your store carry replacement parts? If not, can you order them?"

- "Can you refer me to an authorized repair service?"

- "Who pays for the repair and how?" (Rebate from manufacturer to customer, for example.)

- "Will your store replace items that are still covered by warranty?"

- "If the manufacturer replaces the item, does it have to be shipped? How long will this take?"

skill practice: commonly asked warranty questions

Directions: Be prepared to answer the questions customers ask most often about warranties and warranty items. If you are working in a retail position, answer the following questions about how your store handles items returned under warranty.

If you are not currently working in a retail position, research how your favorite store handles warranty situations by asking these questions about a potential purchase or a purchase you have recently made. This will not only provide you with valuable information, it will provide examples of how you might respond to similar questions when you begin your career in retail.

1. **Does the store handle repairs to items under warranty?**

   ❑ Yes   ❑ No   ❑ **Sometimes** (explain below)

   _____

   _____

   If yes, is the repair work done by the store or is it sent to a repair service?

   ❑ Yes   ❑ No   ❑ **Sent out**

   How long does it normally take for repairs? _____

2. **Does the store sell replacement parts?**

   ❑ Yes   ❑ No

   If not, can the store order replacement parts for customers?

   ❑ Yes   ❑ No

3. **Does the store refer customers to manufacturer-authorized repair services?**

   ❑ Yes   ❑ No

4. **Does the customer ever have to pay for repairs that are covered by warranty? (for example, would the customer have to pay an authorized repair service and then request reimbursement from the manufacturer or from the store?)**

   ❑ Yes   ❑ No

   If so, in what situations would the customer have to pay?

   _____

5. **Will the store replace items that are still covered by warranty?**

   ❑ Yes   ❑ No

6. **Will the customer have to request replacement directly from the manufacturer?**

   ❑ Yes   ❑ No

7. **If the manufacturer replaces the item, how long will it take?** _____

Warranties may or may not be a big part of your job as sales associate, depending on the type of products and services you sell. But understanding the information in Lesson 15 will help prepare you to work in any retail environment. This creates opportunities for you as potential employers discover they can place you in a variety of situations or departments.

Warranties are not the only thing that will bring customers and their purchases back to your store. A sales associate should understand the store's return policies and be prepared to help customers with returns. You'll learn more about return policies in Lesson 16.

LESSON 16

Know Your Company's Return Policy

As you've just learned, the sales associate is a critical link between the customer and the manufacturer when it comes to product warranties. If the warranty is not handled properly, the relationship between the customer and the retail store can suffer. This applies to non-warranty return situations as well. How a store—in effect, *you*—handles returns has a lasting impact on customer relations. Each company has specific policies, some of which may limit you in terms of the authority you have to honor a return. However, every company wants its customers to be happy when they leave the store, even when they are returning a purchase.

Receive returns graciously . . . Sometimes, despite the best efforts of a salesperson, a customer winds up with the wrong item and brings it back. Whatever your company's policy, you will want to welcome the customer warmly and make as graceful an exchange or return of merchandise as possible. Any hesitancy or guilt the customer might have had about returning the item is erased and a long-term relationship is created.

The Importance of Accepting Returns Graciously

After a couple left a hardware store, the husband asked the wife "How much did we pay per gallon for the interior paint?" When she told him, he answered, "That's too much. Let's go back to the store and tell them about the mistake."

When they returned to the paint counter at the hardware store, the couple was told they had been supplied with the $15-per-gallon paint rather than the $11-per-gallon variety. They said they had intended to buy the less expensive paint.

"Why didn't you tell me in the first place?" the salesperson grumbled as he took back the cans and began to mix new paint.

As they drove home with the exchanged paint, the wife said to her husband, "Next time, why don't we try that new hardware store down the road? It's a couple of miles farther, but maybe the attitude will be better there."

Make the policy known . . . Different companies have different return policies, ranging from very strict (absolutely no returns after 10 days; receipt required) to very liberal (returns any time, for any reason; no receipt required). Although the return policy should always be clearly displayed in writing at the point of sale, an important part of your job is to know what your company's return policy is and communicate it to the customer before you finalize a transaction. Even at Nordstrom, a store well known for its liberal return policy, sales associates routinely tell customers at the time of purchase that items can be easily returned if the customer is not satisfied.

Return policies are designed to protect you, the sales associate, your customers and the company by:

- Providing clear guidelines for sales associates

- Specifying conditions for customers (such as no returns on special promotion items, bathing suits, engraved items, or other personalized or intimate items)

- Outlining procedures for processing a return (for instance, receipt required, returns within 30 days, etc.)

"An ounce of prevention is worth a pound of cure." What this old saying advises may be the most important part of building customer goodwill when it comes to returns. By telling your customer exactly what your company's return policy is at the moment of purchase, the customer is well informed and will not be hit with an unpleasant surprise when he comes back to your store to return a purchase.

Know Your Company's Return Policy (cont.)

Returns Can Pay Off in Building Customer Loyalty

The founder of Neiman-Marcus gave his son Stanley some valuable advice early in his career. (Later, this advice helped build Neiman-Marcus into one of the country's most highly regarded stores.) A woman wanted her money back on a dress she had worn once and ruined. Stanley's father told him to refund her money. Stanley objected, arguing that they shouldn't do it since the woman had obviously abused the dress. He also argued that the manufacturer wasn't going to help pay for it.

His father reminded him that the woman wasn't the manufacturer's customer, she was Neiman's. He told Stanley to refund the money with a smile. He also told him that it didn't matter if it cost $200 to get a customer: he didn't want to lose her over a $175 dress. Over time, the woman spent more than a half-million dollars at Neiman-Marcus.

There are different ways to inform your customer about your company's policy, depending on the circumstances. No matter how you offer this information, be sure you are courteous and clear.

> **Example 1 -** *Sales Associate: "I hope your niece likes her graduation gift, but be sure to tell her that we will be happy to exchange it if it doesn't fit."*

> **Example 2 -** *Sales Associate: "You need to know that our store cannot accept a return on these towels if you have your initials monogrammed on them."*

> **Example 3 -** *Sales Associate: "You have found some great values here, but I want to make sure you realize that clearance items cannot be returned."*

Most importantly, give customers accurate information. "I think so," is never good enough—make certain that you *know* so. Be absolutely certain that you are correct in what you are saying. If you are the least bit unsure, check before you speak. Verify information with a co-worker, supervisor, on the computer or in the procedure manual.

Look for alternatives . . . If your company's policy restricts what you can do for the customer—for example, the store will not accept returns on sale merchandise—you will need to treat the customer with absolute respect. Even if a complete refund is impossible, perhaps you will be able to offer something else—a discount coupon, a free sample, or maybe a bottle of a store-brand fabric cleaner that will remove the stain on a recently purchased blouse. Handling the transaction in such a way will make the customer feel you have made every effort possible to help her.

Smoothing the way . . . You may need to direct your customer to a special desk or department that only handles returns. If you behave as a friendly guide throughout this whole process, the customer is less likely to feel inconvenienced by being referred elsewhere. Being the guide also means that you know how to speed things along. If a return form has to be filled out, first know where it is kept and second, volunteer to help fill it out.

CUSTOMER SERVICE

Know Your Company's Return Policy (cont.)

Beyond your authority . . . Finally, if there is a problem you can't solve, you should know who can help and put the customer in contact with that person. Let's say that you've done everything you can to assist a customer returning his food processor, but you don't have the authority to make the exceptions he has asked you to make. Perhaps he doesn't have a receipt (required by your store policy), or has thrown away the original box (your store requires that small appliances must be returned in original cartons). And he has obviously used the processor and damaged it (the plastic blade is chipped).

Be a helpful go-between . . . This is a difficult situation. Your manager or supervisor will probably need to authorize a refund. It may even be that the damage to the blade is a warranty issue, and the manufacturer must be contacted directly to provide a refund or exchange. Even when the decision of whether to accept or decline the return is not up to you, you can still play an important role between the customer and the manufacturer by suggesting approaches and helping the customer to make connections. For example:

Sales Associate: *"You could contact the manufacturer directly for a replacement or refund. I can get the address for you. Or I could get our senior accounts person and see what she might suggest. What would you prefer?"*

Showing that you want to satisfy the customer in whatever way you can, within the limits of store policy, can go a long way in preventing customer complaints and retaining customer loyalty.

skill practice: your store's return policy

Directions: We have already mentioned that it is your responsibility to know exactly what your company's return policy is. To become familiar with it, answer the following questions, noting any additions or exceptions included in the return policy of your store.

If you are not currently working in a retail position, answer these questions about a store in which you frequently shop. This may require that you go to the store and do some research.

Does your customer have to show a receipt?

❑ Yes ❑ No

Does your store only offer merchandise exchanges?

❑ Yes ❑ No

Does your store offer credit-only refunds?

❑ Yes ❑ No

Does your store allow cash refunds?

❑ Yes ❑ No

If the merchandise was a gift, can it be returned without a receipt?

❑ Yes ❑ No

Do you need a manager's approval?

❑ Yes ❑ No

If an item was purchased with a credit card, will your store refund in cash at the customer's request?

❑ Yes ❑ No

What is the policy if a returned item has been discounted since it was initially purchased?_____

_____

Does your store accept merchandise that was purchased from another company's store, if it's an item you carry?

❑ Yes ❑ No

Does merchandise need to be in its original box? (computers, electronic equipment, shoes, etc.)

❑ Yes ❑ No

What do you do if the merchandise looks used or damaged?

_____

_____

Notes:

As you learned in Lesson 16, one of your key tasks as a sales associate is to explain and adhere to your store's return policy. Some stores have very clear and specific rules about returns; others will allow you to use your own best judgment depending on the situation. In either case, it is important to give customers the same attention and respect whether they are making an initial purchase or making a return.

Store policy may put some limits on how you handle returns. However, the way you receive and handle complaints can have an even bigger impact on customer relations than the store's "rules." Handling complaints graciously is a skill all employers (and customers!) will value. Lesson 17 will show you how to use the T.H.A.N.K.S. method for handling complaints.

LESSON 17

Handle Customer Complaints Graciously

Successful companies understand that a customer complaint provides an opportunity to build customer loyalty. When you help to remedy a customer's complaint—whether it's about the unsatisfactory item she purchased, the bad service she received, the inconvenient restrooms in your store, or something else—you are getting two things in return:

- Opportunity Number 1: You are getting an opportunity to turn a customer's bad experience into a good one, thus building a positive customer relationship.

- Opportunity Number 2: You are getting valuable feedback that tells you and your store about problems with products, service, facilities and policies that need to be solved.

> "When customers feel dissatisfied with products and services, they have two options: they can say something or they can walk away. If they walk away, they give organizations virtually no opportunity to fix their dissatisfaction. Complaining customers are still talking with us...So as much as we might not like to receive negative feedback, customers who complain are giving us a gift."
>
> —from "A Complaint Is a Gift" by Janelle Barolow and Claus Moller

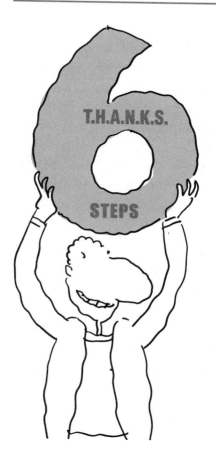

Following these basic steps in handling customer complaints will help you build customer loyalty and open the door for feedback that will help you continue to improve your customer service skills:

T hank the customer for bringing the problem to your attention.

H ear the problem — listen carefully.

A pologize for the inconvenience the customer has experienced.

N eed more information? Ask!

K now a solution and be prepared to propose it.

S olve the problem, or find someone who can.

Handle Customer Complaints Graciously
(cont.)

Thank the customer

Recent studies show that 26 out of 27 customers who experience poor service do not complain. Many people don't complain because they dislike confrontation. Others feel that it is a waste of time, because nothing will be resolved. Some people don't want to prolong their own aggravation by getting into an argument with store personnel. However, once those customers are among friends, family, or co-workers, they don't hesitate to complain about a bad experience. In fact, studies show that unhappy customers will share their complaints with 8 to 20 other people!

So if you view complaints as a chance to improve customer satisfaction and build customer loyalty, doesn't it make sense to thank complaining customers for that opportunity? Thanking the customer for bringing a problem to your attention puts the customer at ease and correcting the problem sends a message that the customer's business is appreciated. As a result, he will probably return to do business with you in the future. Just make sure your "thank you" is sincere and that you take the following steps to correct the situation to your customer's satisfaction.

Hear the problem

Allow the customer to fully explain the problem. When a customer comes to you with a complaint, be prepared to be the best listener in the world. Try to remember that this complaint, no matter how angrily it is given, provides an opportunity for improvement. Keeping this in mind will help you remain patient and sympathetic. Customers are all different in terms of how they behave when they complain: some will be very polite, but unhappy; some will be merely irritated; and some may even be downright angry. But keep yourself focused—you want to get information that leads to a solution.

> " Listen long enough and the person will generally come up with an adequate solution."
>
> —Mary Kay Ash, Founder, Mary Kay Cosmetics

Handle Customer Complaints Graciously
(cont.)

Apologize

When you're dealing with a customer who has no complaint, you begin on positive footing. But when a customer approaches you with a complaint, you will need to regain that positive footing. The first step is to readily apologize for the customer's upset. When you do this, understand that you are not accepting blame. Instead, you are acknowledging the customer's displeasure and inconvenience. You will want to express sincere regret that the customer is unhappy. For example:

Sales Associate: *"I'm sorry the new swing set you bought for your son was broken on his birthday. That must have been very disappointing for both of you."*

Back on track . . . Sometimes your acknowledgment will immediately cool down your customer. You're getting back to the positive footing you will need to reestablish your customer's trust and loyalty. To do this, it is essential that you handle the complaint with as much interest as if it were a sale.

Next, find some point on which you both can agree. Your point of agreement will encourage the customer to cooperate with you in working toward a final resolution or understanding.

Sales Associate: *"I agree. A swing set should last. I'm very concerned that your son's didn't. I want to get this situation corrected so that you and your son can have fun in your new backyard play area very soon. Thank you for bringing the broken swing in with you. That's a real help."*

Whether you're handling a complaint or selling a customer new merchandise, your job is to create a positive relationship that will make the customer a repeat customer.

Need more information? Ask!

If you feel you still haven't heard all the important details related to your customer's difficulty, probe for more information. Try to understand what happened, when, and to whom. Don't worry about the why of the misunderstanding at this point. Instead, encourage the customer to say more by asking questions like "Tell me more about that" or "Walk me through exactly what happened."

Not "Just the facts, Ma'am" . . . Just how do you ask probing questions without sounding like an interrogator? You want to show the customer how committed you are to making things right, so each question should be asked in a friendly way and should yield answers that allow you to solve the problem. For example, the following questions are worded to obtain more information without putting the customer on the defensive. Sometimes it is as simple as letting customers know *why* you are asking for more information, so they won't feel you are questioning their honesty.

- "Did you bring the merchandise with you? If you can show me the bad stitching I can pass the information on to the manufacturer."

- "Can you describe the weird sound? Does it make that noise whenever you use the hair dryer, or just now and then?"

- "This dress has a 40-percent wool content and I have found that many people have allergic reactions to wool fabric. Have you noticed any similar reactions to other items in your wardrobe?"

- "What did the TV screen look like just before the unit started smoking? Did this happen during yesterday's lightning storm?"

Each question will give you important clues in your search to find the best solution to offer your customer.

Handle Customer Complaints Graciously
(cont.)

Need more information? Ask! (cont.)

Expand your customer's knowledge . . . If you have information the customer may not have, share it. As you exchange information, you are reinforcing the customer's understanding that help is on the way! Also, the information you have given your customer will help her think of other possible causes of the problem she's had with her purchase.

Customer: *"I tried using the self-cleaning feature on the oven and it just wouldn't start."*

Sales Associate: *"There is a safety feature built into this self-cleaning model—did you close the oven door with the locking lever?"*

Customer: *"No."*

Sales Associate: *"That's probably it! The self-cleaning can't be activated unless the locking lever has been pulled to close."*

Situations aren't always solved so quickly and easily. But your ability to take the customer through the story of her problem will be one of your strongest tools for arriving at the solution.

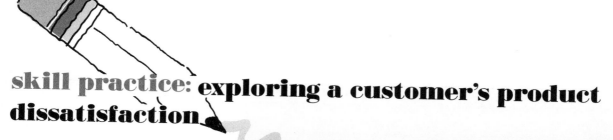

skill practice: exploring a customer's product dissatisfaction

Directions: A customer is returning a suitcase she bought one month ago. Review the following list and check (✓) all of the questions or statements which might be acceptable for helping determine how to help this customer.

❑ Who did you buy this from?

❑ What's wrong with it?

❑ Is the suitcase defective or is there some other reason it did not work out for you?

❑ Do you want a refund?

❑ I'm sorry you are not happy with your purchase. What can I do to make this right for you?

❑ Was this a purchase for yourself or was it intended for someone else?

❑ What methods of transportation will your son be using during his summer in Europe?

❑ Perhaps I can help you find one more suited to your needs...do you still need a carry-on or are you looking for a different size?

❑ Do you have any idea of what caused the handle to break?

❑ What did you do to this thing?

❑ These zippers never break—you must have overfilled it.

❑ How often do you travel?

❑ We have a new line of lightweight, hard-sided bags that are really durable. Would you like to see them?

Compare your answers to those in the back of the book.

Notes:

Compare your answers on page 147 to those in the back of this book. You will notice that how you say something is as important as the words you speak. As you've learned in Lesson 17, handling complaints graciously means treating each complaint as an opportunity to improve. It also means getting enough information to fully understand the nature of the complaint.

The next step in the T.H.A.N.K.S. method gives you the chance to be a creative problem-solver. Being prepared to offer a solution that will meet the customer's needs involves being a good listener, asking the right questions, and knowing what your options are. Lesson 18 will show you how to combine all these skills so you can suggest the best solution for each customer.

LESSON 18

build a continuing relationship

Handle Customer Complaints Graciously
(cont.)

Know a solution

Thanking the customer, listening carefully, apologizing, and asking questions are not enough to regain the trust of a dissatisfied customer. You must also take action to resolve the situation. This begins by finding out what solution would best satisfy the customer. Often, the best approach is to ask her how she would like the situation resolved. This is just plain courtesy. It's also the strongest way to reassure her that you are there to serve her, not to argue with her. Your goal is to keep this customer coming back, not to decide who's right or wrong—either in terms of the problem or its solution.

Sales Associate: *"You paid good money for this purse and I know you expected it to wear better than this. What would you like me to do to make this right for you?"*

Customer: *"Well, I really like the style—do you have any others like it? If not, can this one be repaired?"*

Creative problem-solving . . . Not every customer will have a clear idea either of what she wants or how you can help. In this case, you need to do some creative problem-solving and identify ways to meet her needs.

Sales Associate: *"They have changed the style of this purse slightly and I can show you what we now have in stock. Another option is to have your purse re-dyed and have the strap repaired, at our expense of course. Would you like me to make arrangements for those repairs? If neither of these options appeal to you, I'd be happy to refund your money."*

For customers who do not have a specific request, you'll want to be prepared with your own ideas about the following:

- *What does the customer want?* Have you listened carefully enough to her complaint that you have detected possible solutions?

- *What are the options?* Can you replace the item or repair it? Refund the customer's money?

- *Can you do it?* Do you have authority to carry out the best solution? Do you need a store manager's approval?

- *Is there a reasonable alternative if you can't do what the customer wants?* Do you have a comparable brand-name product that will substitute for a returned item that's been discontinued?

- *Can you offer product care information?* Does your store or the manufacturer have guidelines that will help resolve the customer's complaint, such as a free maintenance guide or a tip sheet of cleaning suggestions?

Remember the golden rule . . . Often, your own shopping experience will tell you what the logical solution should be. Use your best judgment and put yourself in the customer's shoes, then respond as you would like to be treated in a similar situation.

Handle Customer Complaints Graciously
(cont.)

K now a solution
(cont.)

Use good judgment . . . A well-known fast food restaurant instructs associates to ask dissatisfied customers how they would like the situation resolved. Unfortunately, a well-intended associate followed this advice without using his own best judgment. When he delivered a food order through the drive-in window, he did not realize the lid was not properly fastened on the soft drink. The soda spilled all over the customer and her car.

The associate's automatic response was "I'm sorry...what would you like me to do?" Understandably, the customer was angry at such a standard response. How should the associate have responded in this situation?

Here is one suggestion:

Associate: *"I am so sorry. If you'll pull up out of the drive-through lane, I'll be right out with some towels to clean up this mess. I will also bring you a new drink and refund the price of your order."*

If the customer refused this offer:

Customer: *"Oh forget it, I don't have time for this...I am already late for a meeting and now I have to show up with soda all over me."*

Associate: *"My name is Alvin Johnson. Please come back when you are not so pressed for time and let me know what I can do to make this up to you. I would be happy to pay for any dry cleaning expenses resulting from this. And here are some coupons for a free meal. I will be more careful in the future."*

Following the golden rule of treating others as you would like to be treated is generally good advice. But don't make the mistake of assuming what the customer wants. When appropriate, ask first, then be prepared to offer solutions. When the solution is fairly obvious, as in the spilled soda example, don't insult the customer by simply saying "What can I do?"

The exercise on the next page is designed to prepare you for responding to customer complaints effectively.

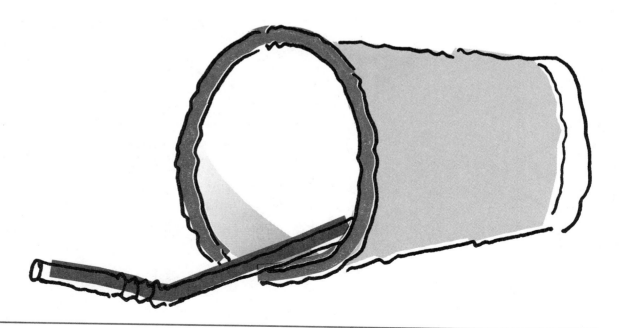

skill practice: resolving complaints

Directions: For each of the following complaint situations, suggest some solution options that the sales associate could be prepared to offer the customer.

SITUATION	SOLUTION
Customer: "I received a call from this store telling me my alterations were ready to pick up. Now that I've come all the way down here and paid for parking, you tell me my order is not ready yet. This is very annoying."	**Sales Associate: "I apologize. Apparently the alterations department did not notice until later that you had two items in your order. We should have called you back to prevent this inconvenience.** **Solution options:** Sales associate might offer to pay for the parking and have the completed order delivered free of charge.
1. **Customer:** "This is not the carpet cleaner attachment I ordered. I even paid extra for rush shipping so I could clean my carpets before my house guests arrive this weekend. Now what am I supposed to do?"	**Sales Associate: "I am sorry for this mix-up. We will do what we can to resolve the situation...what would you prefer?"** **Solution options:** _____ _____ _____ _____ _____ _____ _____ _____ _____ _____ _____

2. **Customer:** "You advertised a special on this item and I went out of my way to buy it from you. Now I find you don't have it in stock...I don't know why I bother to shop at such a disorganized store."

Solution options: _____

_____

_____

_____

_____

_____

_____

_____

_____

_____

_____

_____

_____

3. **Customer:** "I called earlier to ask if you had the new talking teddy bear toy and I was put on hold forever, then I was cut off. What's the deal?"

Solution options: _____

_____

_____

_____

_____

_____

_____

_____

_____

_____

_____

_____

Compare your answers to the suggestions in the back of the book.

Notes:

The solutions you suggested to the situations on pages 154 - 155 probably have a lot to do with your own experiences as a customer. Compare your answers to the suggestions in the back of this book. And when you have the opportunity to handle real customer complaints, remember the golden rule of Lesson 18: respond as you would want to be treated in a similar situation.

You have gone to a lot of work to build customer relationships and handle complaints graciously. Don't blow it all by missing the last step in the T.H.A.N.K.S. method. Lesson 19 will show you how to take action and resolve the problem. This is your opportunity to turn a bad experience into a good one.

LESSON 19

Handle Customer Complaints Graciously
(cont.)

Solve the problem

You have now reached that point in the customer complaint process that determines whether your customer will leave the store feeling good about you and your company. If the customer leaves feeling confident that his complaint has been heard and resolved, he will most likely return for future needs. In fact, he'll probably become the best advertising your company can have. Instead of telling between 8 and 20 people his "horror story" about your store, he will be telling his friends and family what great service he received! But remember, this happy ending requires that you resolve his complaint. It is essential that you follow through on commitments you have made to the customer.

Resolving customer complaints means taking action on what you have learned by listening, asking questions, and giving the customer the opportunity to propose a solution. These are all meaningless gestures if you fail to follow through with a resolution.

Years ago when Marshall Field, founder of a large retail chain, was walking through his original store in Chicago, he heard a clerk arguing with a customer.

He stopped and asked: "What are you doing?"

The clerk answered: "I'm settling a complaint."

Field said: "No, you're not. Give the lady what she wants."

Refunding money . . . If the final solution is a refund, return the customer's money graciously. Count back cash for the customer as carefully as you would if the customer were making a purchase. If company policy dictates that the customer's check must clear the bank before you can give a cash refund, explain that policy carefully and tell the customer when she can expect to receive her refund. If you are processing a refund to a credit account, make sure you follow all the necessary steps and review the paper work with the customer so he is confident that his account will reflect the refund. Always thank the customer for doing business with your company, even if this particular transaction did not result in a final sale.

Arranging for repairs or replacements . . . If additional actions are required to fully resolve the complaint, your work is not yet done. You should keep track of requests for repairs or replacement orders to ensure that the customer is fully satisfied. Do not assume the problem is resolved just because you have sent the product out for repair or ordered a replacement. Check on the request to see that it is completed in a timely manner. If the repair or order is delayed, make sure someone calls the customer to inform him of the delay, or do it yourself. If an item is being shipped directly to the customer, call him shortly after the promised date to make sure it has been delivered and to his satisfaction.

Checking in . . . Some complaints that are resolved on-the-spot may warrant additional follow-up. If the customer was especially upset or inconvenienced, it may be appropriate to follow up with a note or phone call to ensure that he feels the "wrong" has been "righted."

S olve the problem
(cont.)

No matter what the solution is, remember: the basic principles of customer service apply equally to purchases and complaints. You are not resolving the complaint to eliminate an annoyance; you are taking action to retain the loyalty and trust of a valued customer.

Keep records of the customer complaints you resolve, with special notes about methods that worked best. This can be a great help to you when handling similar situations in the future.

When to get help . . . Using the skills you've learned, you will probably be able to solve most of the customer complaints you encounter. However, there are times when skill and diplomacy alone won't be enough. Listening carefully to your customer will help you recognize when it's time for you to seek the support of a more senior store employee.

Depending on your company's policy, appropriate situations to contact management include:

- To resolve very difficult issues

- To communicate to the customer that the matter is important, in the case that your own reassurances are not working

- When the customer is abusive

- When the customer will not otherwise be satisfied

Try to sense when the time is right to call in a manager. Most of all, you want to make sure that you choose this strategy before the situation gets entirely out of hand.

skill practice: you be the judge

Directions: Review the following situations and decide if the sales associate handled the customer complaint graciously ("Yes") or not ("No"). If you feel the response was pretty good, but could have been improved, check "Could be improved."

THE MELT DOWN

Shawn's Situation: Shawn was furnishing his new apartment. Celeste, the sales associate at the import store, spent about 30 minutes helping him find the things he needed. He wrote a personal check for several items, including a set of plastic glasses labeled "dishwasher safe." A sign was posted next to the cash register that stated check-writing customers would only be issued refunds by mail, allowing time for their checks to clear the bank. The next day Shawn returned the glasses, which had melted in the dishwasher, ruining a casserole dish that he had placed next to the glasses on the bottom rack.

Celeste's Response: "I'm so sorry about these glasses, and of course, about your casserole dish. As you say, the manufacturer did not state that you could only put the glasses on the top rack, so this certainly isn't your fault. Thank you for coming back in so we can make this up to you, and also so we can warn future customers about the dishwashing limitations. How would you like to proceed—do you want to try again with new glasses or shall we mail you a refund check?"

Is this a gracious response?

❑   **Yes**   ❑   **Could be improved**   ❑   **No**

THE EGGS-TRA TRIP

Lynn's Situation: As Lynn was putting away the groceries from her weekly shopping at the local market, she noticed the dozen eggs were on the bottom of a bag of heavy items. Sure enough, half of the eggs were broken. After putting away the rest of the groceries, Lynn put the leaking carton of eggs in a plastic bag, got in the car and drove 5 miles back to the market. She stood in line to see Rose, the sales associate who had rung up her items earlier, and explained the situation.

Rose's Response: "Again?! This is the third time that box boy has done something stupid this week. Go ahead and grab yourself another dozen eggs—you don't have to stand in line again—just stop back by here and I'll tag it as paid for so no one stops you going out of the store."

Is this a gracious response?

❑   **Yes**   ❑   **Could be improved**   ❑   **No**

skill practice: you be the judge (cont.)

OUT OF TUNES

Marnie's Situation: Marnie was planning a big party at her new house. Since she would be inviting a lot of people, Marnie splurged on a new 5-disc CD player. She figured that would give her over 3 hours of continuous play, so she wouldn't have to stop and change the music. About 1 hour into the party, the CD player developed a glitch and would not rotate to the next disc unless Marnie manually changed it. She managed as best she could, but the next day took the player back to the store and asked for Leon, the sales associate who sold her the component. She was upset, but explained exactly what had happened and requested a replacement.

Leon's Response: "I'm really sorry this happened—I know how carefully you planned this party. This is the first time I've seen this happen with this model, but I will personally let the manufacturer's representative know about this defect.

"Since the player is under warranty, we will certainly replace it, as you've requested. I realize it's too late to undue the inconvenience this caused you, but I'd like to make this up to you in some way. If you want to replace this with the same model, I'll throw in 5 new CDs, your choice. Or I could upgrade your original purchase and give you the one with the remote feature you were considering earlier; no charge. Which would you prefer?"

Is this a gracious response?

❑   Yes   ❑   Could be improved   ❑   No

Compare your answers to those in the back of the book.

When you have read all of Lesson 19 and completed the skill practice pages 161 - 162, compare your answers to those in the back of this book. As you probably now realize, handling complaints graciously is a skill that improves with practice. You should welcome every customer complaint as an opportunity to improve your skills at providing personalized customer service. And don't forget to use the T.H.A.N.K.S. method!

You are almost finished with Part 3. Just complete the Roundup on the next page—you'll see how much you have learned about providing personalized customer service!

ROUNDUP

Roundup: Build a Continuing Relationship

In this book, you have learned that the relationship you establish with customers should continue even after you have rung up the sale, packaged the purchase, and expressed your sincere thanks. The right attitude and approach to handling complaints will not only build customer loyalty, it will help make a career in retail more rewarding for you. A professional sales associate can take pride in knowing that customers trust and rely on her long after a sale is completed.

The list that follows is a brief roundup of the customer service concepts you have explored in Part 3. Check (✓) the items which you now feel more prepared to accomplish as a sales associate:

- ❑ Help customers understand product warranties

- ❑ Develop expertise about the terms of warranties on products you sell

- ❑ Guide customers through the process of a warranty claim

- ❑ Explain your company's return policy to customers at the time of purchase

- ❑ Handle customer complaints as graciously as you handle the initial sale, using the T.H.A.N.K.S. steps

- ❑ Discover the reasons behind customer dissatisfaction and identify acceptable solutions

If you were unable to check one or more of the items listed above, review the pages related to those topics. And remember that you will be able to refine and improve all of those skills as you build customer relationships on the job. You will learn from your customers as well as your colleagues, as each day brings new opportunities to practice these techniques.

Congratulations!

In Part 3 you have explored methods for extending the customer relationship beyond the initial sale of a product or service. You have learned how to show customers that you and your store stand behind the products and services you sell. This kind of professionalism builds customer loyalty and helps spread the word that you are part of a trustworthy, ethical business. To learn some advanced customer service techniques, continue on to Part 4: *Go the Extra Mile.*

Notes:

part 4

go the
extra mile

Add the Finishing Touches to Your Customer Service

Whether you are just preparing for your first job in retail or you are a seasoned sales associate, there are always additional skills to discover and new techniques to practice. A few of the more advanced customer service skills have been collected in this workbook to get you started on your journey to the next level in your profession.

If you have shopped in stores that practice any of these techniques, you are already familiar with the impact they can have on customers. When a sales associate calls you to make sure you are satisfied with your purchase, it makes you feel important. When you receive a handwritten note thanking you for your business, you know that store appreciates you.

When a sales associate hands you a business card and encourages you to return, you realize someone is always there to help you. When you return to a store and the associate remembers your name, you know you will receive personal attention once again. This is the kind of shopping experience we'd all like to have, especially when we're pressed for time, not finding the items we need, or simply looking for the personalized customer service that makes shopping more enjoyable.

Beautiful Bubbles, Inc.

Dear Ms. VonFeldt,

I just want to let you know how much I enjoyed working with you over the phone to create gift baskets for your staff. I'm sure they will enjoy the products you've selected and they are certainly fortunate to work for such a thoughtful person. If I can be of any further service, either for your employee recognition program or your personal pampering products, please call me directly. I am enclosing our latest catalog with a new line of summer products. Best to you and your company, and thank you again for doing business with Beautiful Bubbles.

Sincerely,

Anne Sloane

Learning Checklist for Part 4

As you complete Part 4, *Go the Extra Mile*, record your progress using the following checklists. These checklists can also be used as a basis for discussion with your instructor, supervisor, or mentor as you complete the skill practices and/or you demonstrate the specific skills in the workplace.

Lessons completed	**Date completed**
❏ Lesson 20: Conduct Customer Follow-up	_____
❏ Lesson 21: Use Business Cards Artfully	_____
❏ Lesson 22: Use Business Cards Artfully (continued)	_____
❏ Lesson 23: Maintain Key Information on Customers	_____
❏ Lesson 24: Offer Personal Shopper Services	_____
❏ Roundup	_____

Learning Checklist for Part 4 (cont.)

Skills Demonstrated in the Workplace	Date Demonstrated

❑   Conduct customer follow-up   _____

Describe the situation and how you demonstrated this skill:

❑   Provide customer with
personalized business card   _____

Describe the situation and how you demonstrated this skill:

	Date Demonstrated
Skills Demonstrated in the Workplace	

❏   Maintain key information on customers   _____

Describe the situation and how you demonstrated this skill:

❏   Schedule personal appointments with
    shoppers; select merchandise in advance   _____

Describe the situation and how you demonstrated this skill:

Notes:

Go the Extra Mile

In this first lesson of Part 4, you will learn how to go the extra mile by following up on customer requests and purchases.

LESSON 20

Conduct Customer Follow-Up

Customer follow-up can occur in a number of ways, and for a variety of reasons. The important thing is to use a method suited to the customer and the situation. In this case, one size does not fit all! Here are a few examples of matching the follow-up method and message to the customer and purchase:

1. Telephone message

"Mr. Stavros, this is Angela at The Well Heeled and I just wanted to make sure your boots arrived. Our records show they were shipped last Friday. If you have not received them by now, or if you have any concerns about your order, please call me at…. If everything is to your satisfaction, no need to call back. Thank you for the opportunity to serve you and I hope you'll come see me next time you need shoes."

2. Thank-you card

"Dear Mrs. Rhodes, I certainly enjoyed helping you select a garden bench for your yard and I hope you are enjoying your morning coffee among the many birds that you mentioned visit your garden. Please come see us again at Gracious Gardens—we loved hearing about your planting adventures. Sincerely, Doug Harper."

3. E-mail

"Dear Ms. Jenks, I just wanted to check in to verify that your new computer desk fit the space you had in mind. Hopefully you are enjoying the new workspace as you read this. If you have further needs for your home office, please call me. Thank you, Glenn Yoshida"

Follow-up etiquette

In addition to matching your method and message to your customers and their purchases, there are some other things you should consider in planning your follow up. The first, of course, is whether you should follow up at all!

To follow up or not . . . Not every purchase requires a follow-up. You needn't call a customer who just bought a ninety-cent pen to see if he's happy with it. On the other hand, if the customer who bought the pen told you he was testing it out to see if he was going to order a large quantity for his office, it would make sense to follow up with him.

Certain types of merchandise—appliances or computers, for example—are costly and can be damaged during delivery. After such a purchase, it is customary for the sales associate to contact the customer to make sure the merchandise was received in good condition—*after* the scheduled delivery date, not before.

You may also want to ask the customer if the store's delivery people were courteous and careful. Their satisfactory performance is also part of what you're selling the customer.

Conduct Customer Follow-Up (cont.)

Follow-up etiquette
(cont.)

Phone savvy . . . Exercise good judgment when conducting telephone follow-up. Not every customer will appreciate one more phone call in his or her busy day, so be sure that the customer's purchase warrants phone follow-up. If it does, consider the most appropriate time and place for that call.

For example, you may have noticed that telemarketers tend to call at dinnertime because they know people are likely to be home. Many customers resent such an interruption (unless they have specifically asked you to call at night).

It might be better to call during the day, leaving a voice message if necessary. In most cases, it is acceptable to leave a message such as the following:

Sales Associate: *"This is Taylor from the Computer Store, and I just wanted to make sure your PC was delivered. I enjoyed helping you select a workstation for your son. No need to return this call if everything is okay, but please call me at 123-4567 if you have any problems with your computer or software or if I can be of further service."*

This leaves the customer in control and does not place an unnecessary burden on him to call you back.

Keep it professional . . . Sending an occasional postcard to your best customers is one very effective—and unobtrusive—way to maintain your relationship with them. While you want to personalize your notes by writing them by hand, you don't want to get personal in a way that would make your customer uncomfortable or that would seem inappropriate. For instance, you can write Rita Lamarr that you hope the wedding shoes she purchased were comfortable during her ceremony. But you don't want to ask her if she had too much champagne at the reception!

Be sensitive about using postcards that others may read. For example, if you are following up on a gift purchase, enclose your note in an envelope.

Conduct Customer Follow-Up (cont.)

Staying in touch

Make it pleasurable . . . The last thing in the world you want to do is alienate your best customers by making a pest out of yourself with too many cards and calls. Staying in touch with customers should be a pleasant, reassuring experience for the customer. A note to a customer immediately following a purchase is acceptable. So are occasional contacts that provide your customer with information she will value—a sale, an in-store promotional event, etc. However, it does not mean camping on the customer's doorstep, leaving a note on the customer's windshield, or visiting the customer at her place of work.

In their best interests . . . Most stores advertise special sales or other promotional events. But customers do not always pay attention to these ads. Customers often appreciate receiving a postcard that informs them of key events, tells them about no-interest charges on store accounts during Christmas, or reminds them of the birthday discount your store offers. It makes customers feel special and shows them that you are looking out for their best interests. A handwritten note from you may also give them that extra incentive to come in.

Valuable contacts . . . This is where knowing your customers and referring to your client records come in handy. Use your client record system to note items your customer asks for and is interested in—even if you are unable to provide them at the moment. The store may get the merchandise in the future, or you may find some alternative merchandise that would suit the customer's needs. Then you can contact the customer. Even if he no longer needs the item, the customer usually appreciates that "you remembered."

skill practice: when to follow up

Directions: Following are a few situations that warrant follow-up with a customer, including one example of the type of follow-up that might be appropriate. For the remaining situations, write in your own ideas of what follow-up might be appropriate.

SITUATION	FOLLOW-UP
Your customer comes in every few months to see if you have any new neckties from his favorite designer.	Write him a note to let him know that you are expecting a new shipment in a week. Offer to hold some for him if he calls you with color preferences.
1. Your customer has purchased an entertainment center and asked to have it delivered and set up in her home.	
2. A customer recently returned a golf bag because it did not have all the features he wanted. You have just found one in your catalog that might fit his needs.	
3. The customer has been waiting for some specific new books to become available. They have finally arrived.	
4. A customer has been in several times to look at wallpaper and has taken samples home but can't decide. You just found out one of your suppliers is sponsoring a wallpaper clinic, to be conducted by a noted decorator.	

Compare your answers to the suggestions in the back of the book.

Notes:

Compare your follow-up ideas for the situations presented on page 179 to those in the back of this book. Yours may not be exactly the same as our suggestions, but they should match the needs and preferences of the customer, a key point in Lesson 20.

Going the extra mile often requires establishing more than a first-name relationship with a customer. In order to take advantage of your personalized customer service, a customer will need to know your full name and how to reach you with a special request. This is where business cards come in handy. Lesson 21 provides some ideas for how to create and use business cards.

LESSON 21

Use Business Cards Artfully

Today, many people exchange business cards when making introductions. This is an effective and efficient way to share basic information such as your name, phone number, and job title. If your company provides business cards, you can use them to suggest to customers that they contact you personally for future needs. If your company does not provide business cards, you can write this information on the sales receipt, special order form, or note card. Use the following tips to make this exchange most effective.

The power of a card ... Your business card not only tells the customer who you are, it also tells the customer that you are serious about your work. While not all stores provide sales associates cards with their own names printed on them, most have store business cards on which you can write your name, department, telephone extension or other information needed by the customer. Such additional information might include:

- Tips for the use and care of a purchase

- Item ordered and date when a special request should be fulfilled

- Name and location of a recommended repair shop or other service

- Directions to the warehouse for a pickup

- Reminder of an upcoming sale or other promotional event

When you give a customer your card, make certain you write down the hours the store is open, and the times during the week when you work. You may also be able to offer an e-mail address or a pager number that will give customers quicker, easier access to you. By doing this, you emphasize your interest in continuing to be of service.

If your store does not provide business cards...

- Write your name and other information on the sales receipt.

- Write a quick thank you note on store stationery and staple it to the receipt.

- Write "Hope to see you at our Anniversary Sale" on sale flyer or postcard, sign your name, and put it in the bag with the purchased item.

- Write "Call me if you have any questions" on the assembly instructions and add your name and phone number.

- Make your own business cards!

Turn the page to learn more about making your own business cards!

Business Cards for Under $20

If your store does not provide business cards for you to use, one option is to make your own! Just check with your employer first to make sure this does not violate any company rules.

Having a personal business card is a great way to say "I am dedicated to serving my customers." Here are just a few ideas for creating your own cards that will cost you less than $20 for as many as 250 cards.

Business card stationery

You can buy paper that is already perforated so you can cut or tear it into the size of business cards. The perforations are very fine, so the result is a smooth-edged card. This paper also has colored designs already printed on it, so you get an attractive, eye-catching card. The paper costs less than $15 at stationery, paper, or office supply stores.

The paper is designed for use in computer printers, so you can make them on your home or school computer or ask a friend to make them for you. Most public libraries now have computers and printers which you can schedule to use free of charge.

Quick print shops

Small, local shops specializing in rapid, inexpensive printing services are a growing business. You can find at least one of these even in small communities; in large cities there seems to be one on almost every block. These shops offer special deals to print business cards for as little as $20. For this price, you can have your name, address, phone number, job title, even a slogan, printed in black ink on white card stock. Many also allow you to include a graphic from the shop's selection of clip art, for no extra charge. Clip art is small drawings, icons, or other images that are computer-ready and easy to add to any computer-generated document. You can select an image that reflects the kind of product or service you sell or one that reflects your personal values about customer service.

simple type created on a computer or by a quick print shop

Bob Collings
Sales Associate
993-8822

Monday - Friday
8:00 a.m. - 4:00 p.m.

clip art

Heel & Toe Co.
111 Main Street
Kansas City

Leo Matlin

Third Avenue Auto Parts

220 NE 3rd Avenue
Spokane, WA
455-9991

pre-printed border

Angela Flowers

12201 S. Broad St., Honolulu, HI 96815
Phone (808) 884-4411 • Fax (808) 884-4412

paper with pre-printed image

PARTY SUPPLY

Jody Plemel
Sales Associate

123 E. Lander, Watertown, MA
Ph: 926-3344 / fax: 926-3445

skill practice: design your own business cards

Instructions: Using inspiration from the examples on the previous page, design a business card you could use in your job. If you are not currently working in a retail position, imagine the ideal job for you and design a card for that.

Your card should have the following information on it:

- Your name and job title

- Your company's name (optional)

- Address and phone number

- A slogan, either for your store or for you personally

Include an image—a border design, a logo, illustration, or cartoon, that would tell your customers something about you or about the products or services you sell.

Hint: look through magazines, the telephone directory, and the newspaper for ideas.

Now that Lesson 21 has you thinking of business cards as your own personal "calling card", there are some things you need to know about the etiquette of presenting and requesting cards.

There are certain " rules" of etiquette in using business cards, as you will discover in Lesson 22.

LESSON 22

Follow the "Rules" of Business Card Etiquette

Offering your business card to the customer

First time's the charm . . . If possible, make sure the customer has your business card before he leaves your store for the first time. However, don't "lead with your card." Help the customer find what she is looking for, complete the transaction if one results, and *then* offer your card and future services. Or you may simply attach your card to the sales receipt and encourage your new customer to call if you can help her again.

You can also offer your card to a customer who is just considering an item and wants a day or two to make a decision. That card is your customer's reminder that when he is ready to buy, you're ready to serve him.

Keep it clean . . . Your business card is a reflection on you, so make sure it projects a professional image. Never give a customer a card that has been folded, has fingerprints or lipstick smudges, or has handwritten notes on it that are not specifically intended for that customer. Keep an adequate supply on hand, preferably in a card holder or box where they will stay clean.

Staying in touch . . . Any time you send a note to a customer, whether it's a thank you note or a notice of a forthcoming sale, be sure to enclose your card. It can have the same power as your signature in terms of reminding your customer of the special service you deliver. It also says "Don't forget to ask for me again."

Unless customers ask for several, offer them just one of your business cards. If you hand them more than one card, they might think you're asking them to distribute your cards to other potential customers. You want to keep the emphasis on person-to-person contact.

Accepting the customer's business card

You first . . . A good rule of thumb is never to ask for a customer's business card unless you've offered your own card first. And keep in mind that many customers will not have business cards; others may not be comfortable using them for personal business.

Some reasons that you might ask for business cards, or simply customer contact information, include:

- A customer is asking about performance of a product; you have offered to research it.

- You mention an upcoming sale and the customer shows interest; you offer to remind her.

- The customer is disappointed that you are out of a specific item; you offer to call him when a new shipment arrives.

- You cannot solve a customer's problem, but you offer to give it further thought and call her back if you think of something.

- An item needs to be altered or customized; you promise to contact the customer when it is ready for pickup.

In other words, if your reason for requesting a card has direct benefit to the customer, then go ahead and ask. But don't just randomly collect business cards to create a potential client list. The customer may see this as pushy or a threat to his privacy. Some experts on business manners even advise that if the person you're helping holds a significant business position (you happen to know she's president of the bank across the street), you should *always* wait for the customer to offer her card, rather than ask for it.

Follow the "Rules" of Business Card Etiquette (cont.)

Treat the gesture with respect . . . When a customer does give you her business card, don't just shove it in your pocket. Look it over with interest. At least use the person's name to indicate you've read it ("Ms. Jones," unless she says "Call me Susan"). You might also add, "Oh, we do business with your bank" or "How was your commute from downtown this evening?" If nothing else, you could compliment the logo or other design element. The point is, you're taking time to show that you are honored to receive the card and you're paying attention to what it tells you about the customer. Also consider that if you put the card in your purse or wallet, the customer may worry you have personal intentions. It would be better to place it in a card file, daily planner, or your client record system.

Make the card count . . . If a customer hands you a business card, use it as a reference card. Jot down a few notes about the customer and his preferences, special requests, or other information that will help you serve him later. If you're keeping a client record, as we suggest next, you can transfer those notes to it later. That way, you can contact the customer if something comes in that might interest him.

If a customer's business card includes a pager number or e-mail address, be sure to ask if it is okay to use these methods for contacting him.

skill practice: the art of the card exchange

Directions: Which of the following examples follow the proper etiquette for requesting or offering business cards? Check (✓) only those which you feel are acceptable.

❏ **Sales Associate:** "I've enjoyed helping you select a wedding gift for your nephew, Mrs. Allen. Here is my business card in case I can be of any further assistance. Feel free to call me directly if you have any questions or special requests. Thank you, and enjoy the wedding!"

❏ **Sales Associate:** "Well, if you change your mind and do want some help, here's my card. Just tell the other sales people that I am already helping you."

❏ **Sales Associate:** "I'm glad I was able to help you find what you needed today. Here are a few of my cards—be sure and tell your friends and family about me."

❏ **Sales Associate:** "I'm sorry we don't carry that brand, but I think you'd be just as happy with the new model we have on order. If you have a business card, I could call you when it comes in."

❏ **Sales Associate:** "I agree you should give this some more thought if it is not exactly what you had in mind. Here is my card in case you think of any additional questions. In the meantime, if you'd like for me to keep an eye out as we get new shipments, I'd be happy to take your number and call you if I spot anything closer to your description."

❏ **Sales Associate:** "We don't have business cards here, but if you'll give me yours I will call you whenever something interesting comes in."

❏ **Sales Associate:** "I'm sorry I don't have a personalized business card to give you, but I've put my name, phone number, and the hours you can reach me on your sales slip—don't hesitate to call me if you have any questions about your new purchase."

Compare your answers to those in the back of the book.

Notes:

Compare your answers for the skill practice on page 191 to those in the back of this book. As you learned in Lesson 22, business cards can provide a starting point for building an on-going relationship with customers. Once you have exchanged this basic information, you will want to establish an organized method of adding to it as you learn more about your clients' needs and interests.

In Lesson 23 you'll learn how to establish a system for recording key information about your clients. This is a "living document" that you should constantly refer to and update as new information evolves.

LESSON 23

Maintain Key Information on Customers

Few salespeople can instantly recall everything they need to know about a customer when he walks back into a store—even if he's a frequent shopper. If you want to succeed in offering great personal service to customers, you will rely on maintaining a record of needs, preferences, and other information that customers willingly share with you.

Keeping a client record . . . This will be your method for recording information about customers. You may want to start with friends and family members who may become your frequent customers. This record system will contain basic information that allows you to stay in touch with your customers. It will also contain specific information that helps you to deliver personalized assistance, such as notifying your customer when you see a new item come into the store that might be of interest to her. Let's say you have a customer who buys large quantities of a high-priced brand of panty hose twice a year. You will become her favorite sales associate, someone she depends upon, when you call her, send her a postcard, or e-mail her to let her know when there's a 20-percent discount on this brand.

Your client record system may be a notepad, a computer file, a card file, a folder, or a simple three-ring binder with a separate page for each customer. Use the type of recording system that works best for you. The important thing is to collect information and keep it up-to-date.

Sample Client Record

Office Objects, Inc.
"we make your business our business"

Sales Associate: _____ Kim _____

Customer Name: _____ Mr. Flanders _____

Work phone: __ 327-2375 ___ **FAX:** __ 327-2300 ____

Company Name: __ Tech Trainers _____
Mailing address: __ 1000 Union St., Suite 400 _____
_____ Fairhaven, CT 08118 _____

Type of Business: _ Business Training _____

Special Requests:
3/5/97	Looking for 10 bin paper organizer for document storage, white, no larger than 3' H x 4' W
4/3/97	Found in Spring '97 catalog, item # 557-9805, $59.99. Called customer and ordered
12/11/98	bought new MP5000 printer and one extra cartridge
2/15/98	ordered additional cartridge; high volume use—notify of cartridge specials.

Special Services:
4/18/97	Had paper bin delivered and assembled.
2/15/98	Placed on mailing list for sale notification.

Maintain Key Information on Customers (cont.)

What to record . . . You can begin by recording information about potential customers—friends and family, even people who come into your store but don't buy anything. If they are looking for a specific item but don't find it, make a note about their request in case you can help them later. Record any purchases your customers make so you can begin to understand their shopping habits. In addition, use this record to keep track of your follow-up activities. Include notes about any sale notices, coupons, thank you cards, promotional announcements, invitations to demonstrations or workshops, etc., that you've sent to each customer. If you know certain customers have responded to your special notices, make a note of that as well. You will remember to include them in future special activities. Some professional sales associates try to recognize special dates in the lives of their customers, such as birthdays and anniversaries, with a card or special offering.

Basic ingredients . . . Your client records should contain the following basic information for each customer:

- Name

- Address

- Telephone

- Occupation (or hobbies, collections, activities, projects, or other interests that influence buying preferences)

Next, add information that will help you to maintain a current profile of the customer's personal preferences and needs. For example:

- Date and type of first purchase or contact. What was the customer shopping for? Did he or she buy anything?

- Preferences or specifications. Are there size variables by brand name or type of item? Color or style preferences? Label or brand-name preferences?

- Special considerations. Is your customer allergic to certain fibers? Does she travel a lot? Does he work the night shift?

- Does your customer prefer to have goods delivered? Assembled? Serviced regularly?

Reviewing to discover opportunities . . . You will want to review the information in your client records regularly. New opportunities may suddenly arise. For instance, your notes say that John Nesbitt has been looking for a recliner that doesn't look like a recliner. One has just arrived in your department. This is your opportunity to shine as the most thoughtful sales associate he's ever encountered. You may also have new ideas of ways to help customer Della Moore improve the efficiency of the home office she is setting up—you've just found a desktop shelving system that has everything!

Maintain Key Information on Customers (cont.)

Keep it new . . . As you've probably guessed, your collection of customer information is a "living" record. Customers' preferences, needs, sizes, etc., may change considerably over time. Just as you keep up with friends and family, it will be vital for you to keep up with your return customers. Record every new bit of information you receive—whether it's that Sally Mason has moved from the city to the suburbs, Joe Pascal is now self-employed instead of a corporate guy, or Maria Martinez has decided she never wants to wear black again.

> **The only person who behaves sensibly is my tailor. He takes new measurements every time he sees me. All the rest go on with their old measurements.**
>
> —George Bernard Shaw, English playwright and author

Keep it confidential . . . Privacy is important to everyone. As a sales associate, you may learn some very personal things about your customers. Be careful about what you say to others. Even such information as dress size or birth date is very personal. Never leave your client records on the counter. Check with your manager to see what the store policy is about storing this information; perhaps a locked cabinet or individual locker can be provided.

It is not up to you to decide what information about the customer should or should not be private. Keep all information that you gather about your customers confidential. Do not share customer information with anyone—even co-workers— without the customer's knowledge and permission. A customer will have more confidence in you if you respect his privacy.

Types of confidential information that you may learn and should never share without the customer's permission:

- Home address and phone number
- Credit card numbers
- Times the customer is or is not home to accept a delivery
- Sizes
- Birth date
- Occupation or place of business

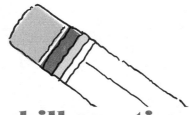

skill practice: creating a client record

Instructions: Using this template, begin creating a client record by noting as much information as you can about one of your customers.

If you are not currently working as a sales associate, practice creating a client record by gathering information about someone you like to shop for—perhaps someone for whom you buy birthday, holiday and special occasion gifts.

Additional copies of this form are included in the back of this book. Use them to begin creating your client record system.

---

c o n f i d e n t i a l

Client Profile

Name: _____

Address: _____ **Phone**: _____

City/State/Zip: _____ **Birthday**: _____

Work: _____ **Title**: _____

E-mail: _____ **Fax**: _____

Contact Restrictions/Requests: _____
_____

Personal Profile (preferences, sizes, etc.):
_____
_____
_____
_____
_____
_____
_____

Buying History:
_____
_____
_____
_____
_____

Recent Requests/Status:
_____
_____
_____
_____

The client record system you learned about in Lesson 23 will help you gain speed in your efforts to provide personalized customer service. Once your customers learn that you are attentive to details and pay attention to their needs, they will turn to you whenever they have special shopping challenges.

Lesson 24, the last in this book, explains the steps for providing personal shopper services. This is where going the extra mile really pays off in building customer loyalty.

LESSON 24

Offer Personal Shopper Services

One of the most satisfying and creative ways of serving a customer is when you act as a personal shopper. Not only does this give you some interesting challenges in terms of testing what you know about your customer's needs and preferences, but it also offers you and the store a special opportunity to be *the* store, *the* sales associate that knows how to give personalized customer service!

Creating confidence

When you act as a personal shopper, the ability to understand the customer's needs is absolutely essential. As you learned earlier in this book, the successful sales associate learns by observing, asking skillful questions, and paying attention to customer clues. You may not always have an established relationship with someone who enlists you as a personal shopper. But that customer will expect you to come up with options that suit her personally. If you don't, then you have wasted the valuable time she was trying to save by having you make selections for her. Your best tools for this job are *listening* carefully to what she says, *writing* yourself some notes so you don't forget, and then *selecting* only items that fit her interests.

Tune in to the customer . . . A customer you have just met has asked you to pick out some clothes for her tropical vacation. Rather than search through the racks herself, she has asked you to find the best choices for her needs. Then she'll come by at a scheduled time to make the final selection. If this was a return customer, you would probably have notes in your client record about her likes and dislikes—colors, size, style, brands, etc. Since you have just met this customer, you'll need to remember everything you observed and heard her say, such as:

Customer: *"I don't like skimpy or see-through resortwear. And I'm not crazy about pastel colors. I like clothes that are comfortable, yet elegant."*

What You Know: *(1) probably prefers conservative lengths in skirts and shorts; (2) nothing transparent or gauzy; (3) pick classic neutrals or dramatic seasonal colors; (4) simple lines and coordinated sets for an elegant look—possibly elastic waistbands, loose-fitting styles.*

You might ask a few questions to clarify the color and style issues, and you should probably ask her what kind of activities she'll be participating in—such as sports, formal dinners, or just relaxing by the water. Most customers won't be upset if you aren't 100-percent successful in meeting all their needs—if you come close, they'll appreciate your efforts. But if you're way off base, they'll lose confidence in you.

Offer Personal Shopper Services (cont.)

Scheduling appointments

Over time, you will collect valuable information from your return customers not only about their merchandise preferences, but about items they're hoping you will eventually have in stock. For example, you may have a customer who collects imported crystal figurines. She appreciates knowing when each new shipment arrives, since the quantities are limited and she's a collector. You know that you should contact this customer immediately when new shipments of the figurines arrive. You also reserve pieces for the customer that you feel will be good additions to her collection.

Schedule individual appointments for such customers. That way, you can attend to each customer according to his or her needs.

Keep your appointment schedule in a book or some portable format, so you can carry it with you. That will help you prevent scheduling conflicts, in both your personal and professional life. By keeping your appointment book with you, you can also contact customers if an emergency comes up and you have to reschedule.

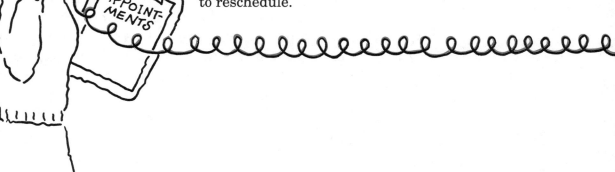

Write down the name and telephone number of the customer and the time and purpose of the appointment. If the customer is shopping for a particular item, write down what it is and all the important details. The day before the appointment, call to confirm the date and time.

Accommodations count . . . Go in a little early or stay a little later if that is what is needed to meet your customer's needs—and if your store policy allows this. Or trade hours with a co-worker who is working on a day your customer wants to shop. The point here is that a special effort on your part may be well worth your while—not just for one sale, but for the many that will likely follow.

TIP

Scheduling Personal Shopper Appointments

Here are some situations where you might want to schedule an appointment with a customer:

- **To show your customer items you've pre-selected, at her request.**
- **You have a special customer who likes undivided attention, even when she is "just looking"**
- **Your customer has a busy schedule and is always in a hurry**
- **A customer relies on you to help him select all of his gift purchases around certain holidays and family events**

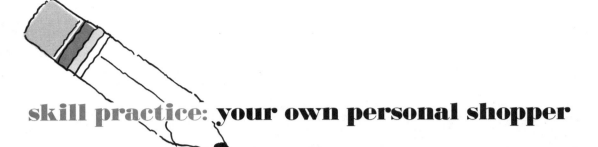

skill practice: your own personal shopper

Directions: Personal shoppers have to be very tuned-in to what their customers are looking for. To increase your ability to tune in to customer requests, pretend that you are planning a dream vacation and need some help getting prepared. This vacation should be designed around your interests—a pampered week at a spa, an outdoor adventure, a month trekking around a foreign country, or a visit to a sports-oriented resort—you pick!

Now make a list of all the things you'll need to buy and write down what your personal shopper will need to know in order to select just the right items for you.

Be specific—this sales associate has never met you before. For instance, you may need to provide guidance on things like brands, quality, colors, sizes, how many, etc.

Your dream vacation:

_____

_____

_____

_____

_____

_____

_____

_____

What you need from your personal shopper:

_____

_____

_____

_____

_____

_____

_____

_____

_____

_____

_____

_____

Once you have followed the steps in Lesson 24 and established yourself as personal shopper for special clients, keeping commitments and following up will be more important than ever. Remember: clients are trusting you to save them time; if you don't do your homework, you are wasting their time, not saving it.

You are almost finished with this book. Just complete the Roundup on the next page—you'll see what an expert you have become at providing quality customer service.

ROUNDUP

Roundup: Go the Extra Mile

In this section, you have learned the value of going the extra mile for your customers. You have also read about some ways that you can go that extra distance that sets you apart from the competition. When customers begin to rely on your knowledge and appreciate your personalized attention, they may become clients for life. They may even seek you out if you change jobs, knowing that they can trust you to treat them well.

The list that follows is a brief roundup of the customer service concepts you have explored in Part 4. Check (✓) the items which you now feel more prepared to accomplish as a sales associate:

❑ Follow-up with customers to make sure they are satisfied with their purchases

❑ Match your follow-up method and message to the individual customer

❑ Observe certain rules of etiquette when conducting customer follow-up

❑ Recognize when follow-up is warranted and when it is not

❑ Use business cards to build a relationship between you and your customer

❑ Create your own business card that tells customers you are a professional

❑ Create a client record

❑ Keep client information confidential

❑ Offer personal shopper services and be prepared to select options that meet customer needs

If you were unable to check one or more of the items listed above, review the pages related to those topics. You may want to practice some of these techniques and ideas on your friends and family to build your confidence and prepare you for going that extra mile with your customers.

Congratulations!

You have completed *Providing Personalized Customer Service*, part of the *Retailing Smarts* series. You should now have basic knowledge and some experience in the national retail skill standards for customer service.
These skills will serve you well as a retail professional or in any position that involves working with customers.

Notes:

answer keys

answer key: you be the detective (page 31)

CUSTOMER CLUE

The customer is picking up every object on one particular display, seemingly comparing the items to each other. — **B**

A man is casually browsing and picking up items that might be for a woman. — **D**

The customer heads straight for one display, looks briefly and then begins to leave the store. — **A**

The customer keeps picking up and then putting down the same item, seemingly unable to make a decision. — **F**

The customer walks in with a shopping bag from your store, goes directly to particular display and begins searching for something. — **C**

The customer gets a shopping cart, pulls out a shopping list and begins going up and down each aisle slowly. — **E**

SALES ASSOCIATE RESPONSES

A. Say "I'm sorry you didn't find what you were looking for…perhaps I can help?"

B. Comment "We just got those in —aren't they lovely?"

C. Say "Can I help you with a return or exchange?"

D. Comment "Looks like you are considering a gift—is there a special occasion?"

E. Comment "Let me know if you need help finding anything."

F. Say "You seem undecided…have you used that product before?"

answer key: opening doors with open-ended questions (page 36)

Your answers will probably vary from the suggestions provided here, but check to be sure your responses are open-ended questions that invite customers to "tell you more" about their shopping needs and preferences.

DEAD-END	OPEN-ENDED
• Did you see our coupon specials?	What brings you into our store today?
• Do you like 100 percent cotton?	What fabric content do you prefer?
• Do you prefer do-it-yourself	How do you feel about do-it-yourself assembly?
• Is this all for you today?	What else can I help you with today?
• Have you read this author before?	What kind of reading material are you looking for?

Your answers will probably be different from these examples, but they should be worded so that customers will feel comfortable discussing their needs with you.

	CUSTOMER	SALES ASSOCIATE
1.	"I was hoping you had some new items for my collection."	Oh, you collect these! Aren't they great? And we are getting a new shipment this week. Which ones do you need to round out your collection?
2.	"I'm looking for a hair dryer."	Are there any particular features that are important to you?
3.	"I need a birthday present for a co-worker."	Great! Is this going to be from the group or you personally? Did you have anything special in mind? Tell me a little about your colleague...does he or she have any hobbies or collections?
4.	"I'm just looking, thanks."	No problem...enjoy yourself and let me know if I can be of any assistance. You look like a baseball fan...do you think they'll win the game tonight?
5.	"I need a better tennis racket."	I'm working on improving my game, too. What are you looking for from a new racket? What don't you like about the racket you are currently using?
6.	"I need a new shirt."	I'd be happy to help you select one...what type of shirt do you have in mind? Is this for a special occasion? What brand of shirts do you usually buy?
7.	"Where is the perfume department?"	It's near the mall entrance to the store. I'm headed that way myself, I'll show you. Are you shopping for yourself or a gift?

Situation 3: A middle-aged man is looking for new seat covers for his 20-year-old car. Your store carries inexpensive vinyl seat covers, expensive sheepskin covers, and several options in between, but you don't know what he has in mind. In fact, you don't know if he is the proud owner of a "classic" or just trying to keep his old "clunker" going.

You might say:

"That car must be a classic...are you the original owner?" or "Do you use this car to drive to work?" or "How often to you drive this car?"

_____

_____

_____

_____

_____

Situation 4: A customer is looking for Italian sausage in your specialty foods store. She does not yet have any other items in her grocery basket, so you can't guess what she is planning to prepare or whether she is shopping for a simple family dinner or a dinner party with lots of guests.

You might say:

"We have several types of Italian sausage...what are you preparing?" or "How many people are you feeding? or "My mother always uses this in her lasagne...are you fixing a favorite family recipe?" or "This is so good...what's the occasion?"

_____

_____

_____

_____

CASE 1: THE SOFTWARE SOLUTION

❑ **Tell Jacob you will call him as soon as the new shipment arrives and put one on hold for him. Who knows, it might even come in later today!**

The choice above would not be the best option for Jacob—he only has two days to get his taxes done and cannot wait for the new shipment, especially since you don't know exactly when it will arrive.

☑ **Ask Jacob what he read in the article that made this program seem ideal to him. Find out more about what he is looking for and see if you have another program in stock that would fit his needs. If not, call the competition.**

This solution is probably the best choice, since Jacob has only recently decided to try using a software program and may not be determined to use only the one he's read about. You may be able to help him pick another program that will work just as well, saving him the time of looking further.

❑ **Call the competition—this man is in a panic and must have that program pronto!**

If Jacob is insistent about buying only this particular software program, then this might be the right solution. However, if the program is popular, chances are he may not be able to find it at another store at this time. Better to try and help him pick an alternative if an acceptable one is available.

CASE 2: THE BURNER ISSUE

❏ **Tell her that the competitor's store may have it in stock, but that you can special order it if she is not in a hurry.**

Find out if she is in a hurry before volunteering the information about the competitor.

❏ **Tell her you don't stock that part and refer her to the competitor's store.**

Since she appears to be getting ready for spring chores, rather than an immediate event (paint, seeds, etc.) and she obviously likes shopping at your store, there is probably no reason to send her to the competition.

☑ **Tell her that you would be happy to special order the part for her and it will arrive in about a week. Then ask if that is soon enough. If she says yes, proceed with the special order.**

This is probably the best solution, based on what you currently know about this customer. If she says she can't wait a week, then of course you should tell her about the competition. But if she is not in a hurry, she will appreciate that you are willing and able to place a special order for her.

answer key: the matching game (page 65)

CUSTOMER SITUATION	LETTER of "MATCHING KINDNESS"
Customer is loaded down with several bags of already purchased items.	B
Customer buys something that is large, bulky, or heavy.	G, E
Customer is hesitating over a purchase.	A
Customer is in no hurry, just wants to browse.	I
A customer is accompanied by an elderly person who appears frail or confused; the companion may appear impatient about waiting.	C
An elderly customer with limited mobility.	F
A person traveling on business or vacation.	H
A mother with a fussy infant.	D

A. Offer to let customer make a local call to verify appropriateness or preference.

B. You can offer to consolidate many small packages into one large shopping bag.

C. Take whatever steps you can to accommodate them immediately, even bending the rules a bit, asking for assistance from a co-worker, or asking another customer to excuse you for a moment while you get this person settled.

D. Let her know if you have a quiet corner or lounge where she can tend to her baby's needs.

E. Offer to temporarily store purchases if customer has more shopping to do.

F. Offer to bring merchandise to the customer while he sits down.

G Offer to deliver the item, carry it to customer's car, or have it available at package pickup.

H. Offer to have packages shipped.

I. Offer a cup of complimentary coffee to make the customer feel welcome.

answer key: provide balanced service (pages 92-93)

1. You should:

☐ Offer to call the phone customer back so you can continue asking the in-store customer more questions.

☐ Ask to put the phone customer on hold and then go back to the in-store customer to see if she needs any help yet.

☑ Help the phone customer now, allowing the in-store customer to browse on her own for awhile.

> Your in-store customer is probably sending you non-verbal clues that she wants to look around. Give her some time to explore your store or department while you help the phone customer, but keep an eye out for any signs that she has a question or needs some assistance.

2. You should:

☐ Ask to put the caller on hold and check on her request as soon as you are done with your current customer.

☑ Explain that you're really busy with other customers at the moment and offer to call her back. This would require stopping what you're doing and writing down her name and phone number.

> This is probably the best option in this situation. Just be sure to excuse yourself to the in-store customer you are helping, assuring that customer that this will only be a momentary interruption. Also, make sure you repeat back the name and phone number and tell the phone customer how soon he or she can expect you to call back. This provides balanced service to all customers involved.

☐ Stop what you're doing and go check on her item immediately, since it won't take long and the phone customer sounds stressed.

answer key: provide balanced service (cont.)

3. You should:

❑ **Offer to call back and discuss the sale item as soon as you are done helping the in-store customer**

☑ **Ask to put the caller on hold while you check on the sale item, stopping on the way to assure the in-store customer you will be back with him in a moment.**

Your in-store customer wants to be thorough and make a good decision; he does not appear to be a hurry. However, since the in-store customer is close to completing the transaction, you don't want to leave him alone for very long. Give the in-store customer a few minutes to review the details of the warranty while you answer the phone customer's question. If the phone customer needs additional help that will keep you away from the in-store customer too long, offer to call back in a few moments.

❑ **Focus on the phone customer; the in-store customer has already taken up enough of your time!**

answer key: **full-service responses** (page 101)

Your responses will probably be different than the suggestions here, but be sure you are giving your phone customers full-service responses—consider what additional information might be helpful to them, based on their questions.

PHONE CUSTOMER

Can you tell me if my prescription is ready?

What is your price on the Reliable Baby Monitor?

How long do custom orders take?

Do your bicycles come already assembled?

SALES ASSOCIATE

Yes, it is ready to pick up now if you like. If you'd prefer, we can deliver that to you by 5:00 p.m. tomorrow, free of charge.

Our price is $25, which we believe is competitive. If you find it for less, we will meet the price. By the way, we have a gift registry service in our baby department, if that would be helpful to you.

Normally, special orders take 2 weeks, but we can have it shipped overnight from the factory for an additional $10.

You have the option of assembling the bicycle yourself or paying an additional fee to have it assembled. We also sponsor an assembly and repair clinic on Saturday mornings, if you'd just like to use our tools and have someone available to answer questions.

answer key: processing special orders (page 113)

Customer: Cramer and Associates

Address: 1004 Fifth Avenue

Phone: 445-3808

ITEM	SIZE	QUANTITY	COLOR/FINISH
bookcase	extra-large	10	pine

Deliver to: ❑ Store   ☒ Customer   **Delivery charge:** $50

Rush Order: ❑ No   ☒ Yes   **Rush fee, if applicable:** $100

SPECIAL INSTRUCTIONS:
Will need to use freight elevator at customer site. Call Rich at 445-3808 extension 103 for access to elevator (he is available 9:00 am - 5:00 pm)

Delivery Date: August 3, between 9:00 am and 5:00 pm

Sales Associate: Camille

answer key: exploring a customer's product dissatisfaction (page 147)

Questions or statements such as those checked (✓) here will put your customers at ease and help you discover how best to meet their needs.

❑ **Who did you buy this from?** (The customer might think you are accusing her of returning something that was purchased at another store. Or she might think you are not going to help her.)

❑ **What's wrong with it?** (This is abrupt and the customer might think you are questioning her right to return the item.)

☑ **Is the suitcase defective or is there some other reason it did not work out for you?**

❑ **Do you want a refund?** (This closed question limits her options and does not give you enough information to help her make another selection.)

☑ **I'm sorry you are not happy with your purchase. What can I do to make this right for you?**

☑ **Was this a purchase for yourself or was it intended as a gift for someone else?**

☑ **What methods of transportation will your son be using during his summer in Europe?**

☑ **Perhaps I can help you find one more suited to your needs...do you still need a carry-on or are you looking for a different size?**

☑ **Do you have any idea of what caused the handle to break?**

❑ **What did you do to this thing?** (This response, and the next one, assume that the customer did something wrong, which may not be the case.)

❑ **These zippers never break—you must have overfilled it.**

☑ **How often do you travel?**

❑ **We have a new line of lightweight, hard-sided bags that are really durable. Would you like to see them?**

answer key: resolving complaints (pages 154-155)

Your solutions may vary from the following, depending on your own experiences and/or the policies of your company.

SITUATION	SOLUTION
1. Customer: "This is not the carpet cleaner attachment I ordered. I even paid extra for rush shipping so I could clean my carpets before my house guests arrive this weekend. Now what am I supposed to do?"	**Sales Associate: "I am sorry for this mix-up. We will do what we can to resolve the situation...what would you prefer?"**
	Solution options: If the customer does not specify a solution, the sales associate could offer to reorder the item and have it delivered directly to the customer the next day. Or if the store has an alternate product in stock (or as a rental service), the sales associate might loan the equipment to the customer until the correct attachment arrives.
2. Customer: "You advertised a special on this item and I went out of my way to buy it from you. Now I find you don't have it in stock...I don't know why I bother to shop at such a disorganized store."	**Solution options:** Apologize, explain why there is an out-of-stock situation (unanticipated response, delivery problems, etc.) and offer a "raincheck" or the substitution of a comparable item at the same discount.
3. Customer: "I called earlier to ask if you had the new talking teddy bear toy and I was put on hold forever, then I was cut off. What's the deal?"	**Solution options:** Apologize, explain if appropriate, but don't make excuses. Ask if you can take the customer's name and phone number so you can check on her request and call her back. Specify when you will call and then do it. Take extra steps to regain this customer's trust, such as putting the item on hold, offering to deliver it, or if you do not have the item, offer to order it or find out if a competitor has it in stock.

THE MELT DOWN

Is this a gracious response?

☐ Yes   ☑ Could be improved   ☐ No

While Celeste was gracious in handling Shawn's complaint, there is room for improvement. Even if she thought she had mentioned it the day before, Celeste should have explained why Shawn would have to wait for a refund check rather than receive cash on the spot. Also, Celeste made no offer to replace the casserole dish. Even if she felt store policy would prevent her from taking such a step, she might have checked with a manager to see what could be done in this situation.

THE EGGS-TRA TRIP

Is this a gracious response?

☐ Yes   ☐ Could be improved   ☑ No

At first glance, Rose may appear to be gracious by saying Lynn does not have to stand in line again, but this is small compensation for the inconvenience the customer has already experienced. At a minimum, Rose should have called the box boy and asked him to get Lynn a new carton of eggs. In this way, Lynn would have been better served and the box boy would have had an opportunity to learn from his mistake. An additionally gracious gesture would have been for Rose to issue a refund for the eggs or a coupon toward Lynn's next purchase.

OUT OF TUNES

Is this a gracious response?

☑ Yes   ☐ Could be improved   ☐ No

Leon apologized and showed empathy for how the situation affected Marnie's party plans. His promise to notify the manufacturer reinforced that Marnie's complaint was valid and appreciated. Since Marnie already told Leon she would like a refund, he did not insult her by routinely asking "how would you like this resolved?" However, Leon did go a step further and offer Marnie more that she asked for, since his store allowed him to use his own best judgment. This told Marnie that she was a valued customer.

answer key: when to follow up (page 179)

Your ideas may be somewhat different from the suggestions here, based on your own experiences and perspective. The important thing is to match your follow-up technique with the needs and preferences of each customer.

SITUATION	FOLLOW-UP
1. Your customer has purchased an entertainment center and asked to have it delivered and set up in her home.	Call to see if the furniture was delivered on time and assembled to her satisfaction. Ask if she was happy with the service. Thank her again for her business.
2. A customer recently returned a golf bag because it did not have all the features he wanted. You have just found one in your catalog that might fit his needs.	Send him the catalog (or a copy of the product information and a picture) with a note that says you thought of him when you saw this item. Offer to order one for him if he is interested.
3. The customer has been waiting for some specific new books to become available. They have finally arrived.	Call the customer to let her know the books are now available. Offer to have them delivered directly to her home or put them on hold for her if she'd prefer.
4. A customer has been in several times to look at wallpaper and has taken samples home but can't decide. You just found out one of your suppliers is sponsoring a wallpaper clinic, to be conducted by a noted decorator.	Send the customer a flyer about the clinic with a handwritten note that says the decorator may be able to help her with her wallpaper decisions. Suggest that you can reserve her a place in the clinic and ask her to call you if she is interested.

answer key: the art of the card exchange (page 191)

Only the examples which are checked (✔) follow the proper etiquette for requesting or offering business cards.

☑ Sales Associate: "I've enjoyed helping you select a wedding gift for your nephew, Mrs. Allen. Here is my business card in case I can be of any further assistance. Feel free to call me directly if you have any questions or special requests. Thank you, and enjoy the wedding!"

☐ Sales Associate: "Well, if you change your mind and do want some help, here's my card. Just tell the other sales people that I am already helping you."

☐ Sales Associate: "I'm glad I was able to help you find what you needed today. Here are a few of my cards—be sure and tell your friends and family about me."

☐ Sales Associate: "I'm sorry we don't carry that brand, but I think you'd be just as happy with the new model we have on order. If you have a business card, I could call you when it comes in."

☑ Sales Associate: "I agree you should give this some more thought if it is not exactly what you had in mind. Here is my card in case you think of any additional questions. In the meantime, if you'd like for me to keep an eye out as we get new shipments, I'd be happy to take your number and call you if I spot anything closer to your description."

☐ Sales Associate: "We don't have business cards here, but if you'll give me yours I will call you whenever something interesting comes in."

☑ Sales Associate: "I'm sorry I don't have a personalized business card to give you, but I've put my name, phone number, and the hours you can reach me on your sales slip—don't hesitate to call me if you have any questions about your new purchase."

client
profile
records

Use the following pages
to begin creating a client
record system. You may
want to remove or copy
these pages and put them
in a notebook for handy
reference on the job.

Client Profile

Name: _____

Address: _____   Phone: _____

City/State/Zip: _____   Birthday: _____

Work: _____   Title: _____

E-mail: _____   Fax: _____

Contact Restrictions/Requests: _____
_____

Personal Profile (preferences, sizes, etc.):

_____
_____
_____
_____
_____

Buying History:

_____
_____
_____
_____

Recent Requests/Status:

_____
_____
_____
_____
_____
_____
_____
_____

confidential

Client Profile

Name: _____

Address: _____ Phone: _____

City/State/Zip: _____ Birthday: _____

Work: _____ Title: _____

E-mail: _____ Fax: _____

Contact Restrictions/Requests: _____
_____

Personal Profile (preferences, sizes, etc.):
_____
_____
_____
_____
_____
_____

Buying History:
_____
_____
_____
_____

Recent Requests/Status:
_____
_____
_____
_____
_____
_____
_____
_____

Client Profile

Name: _____

Address: _____ Phone: _____

City/State/Zip: _____ Birthday: _____

Work: _____ Title: _____

E-mail: _____ Fax: _____

Contact Restrictions/Requests: _____
_____

Personal Profile (preferences, sizes, etc.):
_____
_____
_____
_____
_____

Buying History:
_____
_____
_____
_____

Recent Requests/Status:
_____
_____
_____
_____
_____
_____
_____
_____

Retailing Smarts Available in Workbook Format

Providing Personalized Customer Service

...is also available as a set of four smaller workbooks.

While identical in content to this book, the smaller workbooks are ideal if you only want to learn about a few of these topics. The smaller format can also be used as a quick reference on the job.

The four workbooks are:

> **Workbook 1**: *Get to Know Your Customer* (72 pages)
>
> **Workbook 2**: *Meet Your Customers' Needs* (80 pages)
>
> **Workbook 3**: *Build a Continuing Relationship* (64 pages)
>
> **Workbook 4**: *Go the Extra Mile* (64 pages)

A note to Training Directors:

Let us show you how we can design training materials specifically for your work environment and employees. Crisp Custom Training is a great solution for medium- and large-size organizations.

For more information on books in the ***Retailing Smarts*** series, or hundreds of other topics in easy-to-use, self-study learning materials, and our custom training development contact:

CRISP PUBLICATIONS
1200 Hamilton Court
Menlo Park, California 94025
1-800-442-7477
www.crisp-pub.com.